GOD'S WILL

IT IS WRITTEN

Preston Condra | Kelly Condra

www.sufficientword.com

God's Will
It is Written
Preston Condra and Kelly Condra

Published by Sufficient Word Publishing, a division of
Sufficient Word Ministries, Springdale, AR.
Copyright ©2020 Preston Condra and Kelly Condra
All rights reserved.

Second Edition
Previously published as *God's Will: Read All About It.*

No part of this publication may be reproduced, stored in a retrieval system, or transmitted in any form or by any means, electronic, mechanical, photocopying, recording, scanning, or otherwise, except as permitted under Section 107 or 108 of the 1976 United States Copyright Act, without the prior written permission of the Publisher. Requests to the Publisher for permission should be addressed to Permissions Department, Sufficient Word Publishing, publisher@sufficientwordpublishing.com

All verses are from the King James Version of the Bible unless otherwise noted. Bold text added to some verses for emphasis.

Scripture quotations marked "NKJV" are taken from the New King James Version of the Bible. Copyright ©1982 by Thomas Nelson, Inc. Used by permission.

Scripture quotations marked "NASB" are taken from the New American Standard Bible®. Copyright ©1960, 1962, 1963, 1968, 1971, 1972, 1973, 1975, 1977, 1995 by The Lockman Foundation. Used by permission.

Scripture quotation marked "AMP" is taken from the Amplified® Bible. Copyright © 1954, 1958, 1962, 1964, 1965, 1987 by The Lockman Foundation Used by permission.

Scripture quotation marked "YLT" is taken from The Young's Literal Translation Bible. (Public Domain)

Cover and Interior design: Madison Lux, *upwork.com/fl/madisonlux*

ISBN: 978-1-946245-27-4

Wherefore be ye not unwise,
but understanding what the will of the Lord is.
(Ephesians 5:17)

TABLE OF CONTENTS

Introduction	Only the Truth Sets Christians Free to do God's Will	1
Chapter 1	God Wills that All the World Would be Saved	15
Chapter 2	God Wills that Christians Know Him Through His Word	27
Chapter 3	God Wills that Christians Adopt the Divine Viewpoint	43
Chapter 4	God Wills that Christians Communicate to Him	67
Chapter 5	God Wills that Christians be Filled with His Fullness	83
Chapter 6	God Wills that Christians be Holy as He is Holy	99
Chapter 7	God Wills that Christians Live Extraordinary Lives	123
Chapter 8	God Wills that Christians have Extraordinary Relationships	145
Chapter 9	Suffering and Glory	171
Chapter 10	God Wills that Christians' Lives be Profitable, Now and in the Future	191
Conclusion	What God's Will is Not	209

INTRODUCTION

ONLY THE TRUTH SETS CHRISTIANS FREE TO DO GOD'S WILL

…thou hast redeemed me, O LORD God of truth. (Ps 31:5b)

In a moment of unparalleled irony, Pilate said to Jesus Christ, God clothed in flesh, and the incarnation of truth, "What is truth?" Truth is the reality of things. It is found in only one place on earth: The Bible. The Bible is not merely a container of truth; it is the truth. The world only has facts, and even those are partially known and tend to change. The truth, however, is how things actually are according to the only one who actually knows. Only God can see things as they really are. He is light, illuminating the willing to comprehend those things which He has revealed in His written word.

…thy word is truth. (Jhn 17:17b)

This then is the message which we have heard of him, and declare unto you, that God is light, and in him is no darkness at all. If we say that we have fellowship with him, and walk in darkness, we lie, and do not the truth… (1 Jhn 1:5-6)

Understanding truth enables a certain way of operating; Christians are to "do" truth. To operate in reality, Christians must share God's viewpoint and grasp the content of His revealed will.

What we, the authors, see in the churches is that many saints are willing to operate in the truth, but not many are confident regarding what they are to do. Whether it is taking what amounts to a personality test to determine one's role, or trying to discern feelings and signs, segments of today's universal church seem to have become unmoored from the convictions held by the early church in regard to its mandate. The early church members are not depicted wringing their hands about what to do, or living in anguish, fearful of making wrong decisions. They knew God's will and did it. So too can Christians today.

In our customized culture, perhaps the idea that we all have essentially the same job to do is not very appealing. It is more attractive to imagine a personalized life plan, delivered to the front door by God Himself. This popular characterization of God's will, however, actually undermines the daily relationship between God and His children, creating uncertainty and insecurity rather than boldness and assurance. The neglect of the truth in favor of changeable feelings and contradictory signs robs the Christian of the confidence he should have in His walk of faith; the faith-rest life has morphed into something of a scavenger hunt.

We ask our readers to consider these questions: Apart from general morality such as "do not murder," does the Bible teach that there is only one right choice for every situation? If the Bible did teach this, could it also claim to be complete, fully equipping every saint for "all things pertaining to life and godliness?" After all, it does not contain every possible scenario. How could it instruct millions of people, across cultures and vast expanses of time if every person has a unique, pre-determined, and unknown path? How could it guide us, for example, in regard to things that did not exist in its time? Is there a conflict between the Bible's claim of sufficiency and its lack of exhaustive content? Since it claims to provide all that we need to know, yet it does not instruct us specifically in each of hundreds of daily decisions, what are we to conclude? We, the authors, suggest this: God has things for us to do, and yet we are also free to make choices; our lives are not so tightly circumscribed as to only offer one option per situation.

Part of the difficulty that some experience in trying to discern God's will might be the concentration on figuring out *what* to do. We know that God's way is narrow, but perhaps His way is better explained as a "how" rather than as a "what." For Israel, the narrow way was the Mosaic Law; it ordered the way in which the Jewish people were to live. Similarly, there will be a narrow way under the laws of the Kingdom; Jesus explained these principles to Israel during His earthly ministry. So too, the church has a narrow way; it is called spirituality. We, the authors, believe that a Christian who operates by the power of the Spirit, accessing the freely given wisdom of God, can make many choices which bring Him glory. The "how" of Christian living teaches, trains, and empowers us to do the "what."

If this is not the case, what are we left with? Are we to try to read circumstances as wizards read crystal balls, searching for "confirmation" in a universe full of possibilities? How about going by our feelings, rolling on the waves of emotion in a sea of relativity, trying to judge decisions by a standard which can vary from moment to moment? From a sunny day to a cloudy day, from a happy song to a sad one, from good luck to bad, our feelings rise and fall; they will take us for a ride if we allow them to. Perhaps we should plead with God for answers, but that will leave us wondering why He does not speak. Or is the Bible wrong in its claim to be the final word until Christ's return? Without the certainty offered by God's word, preserved through the ages for us, it is no wonder that for many there is little urgency to do the work of the ministry. A Christian can become paralyzed by the many possibilities, never certain about which "what" he is to do. If God desires a particular action in every situation, but has not provided clear instruction, the bold assurance needed for victorious and productive Christian living is unlikely to be realized.

There is good news, however: GOD HAS SPOKEN. His will has been revealed and can be known. Two thousand years ago the Creator entered time, took on humanity, and proved Himself to be who He claimed. Jesus Christ, the word of God, is the author of a book that contains all things pertaining to spiritual life. Understanding spiritual things provides wisdom and empowerment for physical life. This miraculous book goes even further, informing us how to live a God-honoring life of meaningfulness, satisfaction, and eternal reward. Even better still, these benefits are equally available to the rich and the impoverished, the powerful and the marginalized, the healthy and the sickly, the free and the imprisoned, the young and the old, the new believer and the mature.

Willingness

If any man will do his will... (Jhn 7:17a)

Mandatory to the "how" of doing God's will is willingness. God does not force the lost into heaven; neither does He force the saints into service. We are not forced to pray, attend religious services, read the Bible, or cooperate with His mission for the church. There are Christians everywhere who know nothing and do nothing. That is an option when one is free, and the Bible warns that many will enter the kingdom without an inheritance to claim, unprepared to rule and reign (Heb 6:12). As you read the many aspects of God's will which are described in the following chapters, remember that every person who is born again has the mind of Christ because God indwells his regenerated human spirit (1 Cor 6:17). Every functional Christian is able to learn, understand, and even become willing to do all that that the Father wills.

> *Jesus saith unto them, My meat is to do the will of him that sent me, and to finish his work.* (Jhn 4:34)

> *I can of mine own self do nothing: as I hear, I judge: and my judgment is just; because I seek not mine own will, but the will of the Father which hath sent me.* (Jhn 5:30)

> *For I came down from heaven, not to do mine own will, but the will of him that sent me.* (Jhn 6:38)

> *Then said Jesus unto them, When ye have lifted up the Son of man, then shall ye know that I am* he, *and* that *I do nothing of myself; but as my Father hath taught me, I speak these things. And he that sent me is with me: the Father hath not left me alone; for I do always those things that please him.* (Jhn 8:28-29)

> *Let this mind be in you, which was also in Christ Jesus…* (Phil 2:5)

As He did in initial salvation, God has blessed us with absolutely everything that is needed for our daily lives to align with His will.

He teaches, motivates, empowers, and rewards those who desire to obey and glorify Him. There is only one thing that God does not do for us. He does not open the book. Each of us must open the Bible for ourselves and read it. Through faith, God provides all the rest.

Our Goal

Our purpose in writing this book is to present the major themes of God's will for Christian living, and to offer freedom from the non-biblical idea that there is one choice, one path, or one decision which must be divined in order to please God, a belief that has plagued many saints with uncertainty, anxiety, and fear. Christians have been shamed for making decisions according to what they know and asking God to bless their choice. Yet the alternative to the application of biblical wisdom is to seek signs, judge feelings or practice other mystical methods, none of which are taught in scripture. The prevalent low view of scripture has in a practical way separated Christians from God, turning them instead to untrustworthy experiences. God is not ministering experiences and feelings for use in decision-making; He is ministering the truth through His written word. The Bible's own claim is that it thoroughly furnishes the willing saint unto all good works. Apart from that conviction and practice, no saint can grow in grace, increase his faith, or know his Lord better, as the knowledge and power needed for these things is found only in the Bible. If you, reader, have any doubt that the church has been led astray in regard to the sufficiency of scripture, look at Christianity's impact on the culture and think again.

> *If any man will do his will, he shall know of the doctrine, whether it be of God, or whether I speak of myself.* (Jhn 7:17)

> *Having made known unto us the mystery of his will, according to his good pleasure which he hath purposed in himself…* (Eph 1:9, a mystery was formerly hidden but is now revealed.)

> *Wherefore be ye not unwise, but understanding what the will of the Lord* is. (Eph 5:17)

The verses above do not say, "if you can figure it out," but that God's will is knowable. Life may seem like a mystery, but the Bible declares that we can know what God wants us to, and carry out the purpose He has for human life, which is to glorify Him and enjoy Him forever.

Possible Causes of Confusion

The will of God might seem difficult to understand, and we, the authors, believe there are several reasons for this. Firstly, there seems to be a lack of understanding of how the grace-through-faith system works: believing that one is in a "seeking" relationship with God results in uncertainty. Christians can rest in the assurance that God's will has been revealed and can be understood. Knowing and believing that which is true removes uncertainty.

Secondly, a failure to rightly divide the word of truth creates much confusion; many Christians do not know which scriptures are to be applied to daily living. Simply put, using someone else's program and claiming their promises does not result in a life that conforms to God's will.

A third cause of difficulty regarding God's will is a misuse and overuse of the concept of sovereignty. Sovereignty is a governmental term; God is the ultimate ruler, but Christians are not in a legal/governmental relationship with Jesus Christ. He is the head in a spiritual relationship characterized primarily by love. Extreme views regarding sovereignty portray God similarly to a micromanaging dictator who prescribes every move. Such an idea will naturally lead Christians to seek what that move is to be rather than resting in the assurance that we know what we are to do and how we are to do it.

Fourthly, there is a lack of knowledge about the content of scripture. Across Christendom, scriptural knowledge is at a low point in the modern era. We cannot obey what we do not know.

An Overview of God's Will

> *...always labouring fervently for you in prayers, that ye may stand perfect and complete in all the will of God.*
> (Col 4:12b)

The Christian has been blessed with a large book of instruction. Here are a few examples of God's will for Christians:

- God wills that men believe the Gospel, benefit from the payment made for their sins by Jesus Christ, and share the good news with others.
- God wills that Christians know Him through His word and communicate to Him through prayer.
- God wills that Christians live rightly related to the Holy Spirit, aligned in attitude, motive, belief, and choices.
- God wills that Christians yield to the power of His grace, thereby producing spiritual fruit which reflects His loving, good, and forgiving character.

- God wills that Christians live in accordance with their exalted position in Christ, displaying His virtues through pure and holy lives of moral excellence and high standards.
- God wills that Christians enjoy all that He has provided in liberty, exercising wisdom so that our choices do not become an occasion for the three spiritual enemies to take advantage.
- God wills that the primary recipients of Christian good works are to one another as a remarkable, shining example of family love among those He redeemed, and as an aid so that each can accomplish the work of the ministry.
- God wills that Christians mature, more consistently doing the above, in order to prepare for the responsibilities of the kingdom.
- God wills that Christians sometimes suffer, trusting Him through it in order to be made more perfect for ministry.
- God wills that everything His children do would result in rewards for them and glory for Him.

When we abide as spiritual men, reading and studying God's word and applying it to life, it provides all that is needed for life and godliness, thereby facilitating good works. Blessed assurance! We are not left guessing; we can live confidently in God's will through His sufficient written word.

Using This Book

It has been a formidable endeavor to write about God's will. This book introduces many topics about which an entire book could be written. This volume amounts to a primer on several aspects of Christian living, including spirituality, sanctification (holiness), fellowship, and prayer. It is comprehensive but not exhaustive; for example, it merely mentions widely published popular topics like money, parenting, and marriage. It does not include specific professional topics like pastoral requirements, or topics that require lengthy explanation such as how to conduct spiritual warfare. The subjects covered are best described as some of the major themes of Christian living.

If you are not familiar with living by the power of Spirit-filling, the doctrines presented might seem difficult to understand. We encourage you strongly to persevere in this study! God could have written a leaflet, but instead He gave us a large book. He wants us to persist in our efforts to know Him. Remember, all the doctrine that you know was new to you at some point. Read the Bible verses with faith; God promises to teach them to all who want to know. Paul emphasized the renewing of the mind because every Christian needs to reread and relearn grace doctrine throughout his life. Our enemies never stop trying to deceive us and keep us from learning. Be patient. Spirituality and the maturing process does not happen overnight. Some things will be understandable, and others will take many readings, just as they did for us to learn them. The foundation of spirituality—faith—is an example of something that might need to be re-learned. It is mentioned throughout the book in order reinforce the way in which every aspect of God's will is accomplished in the saint.

This book frequently mentions the saving Gospel of Christ found in 1 Corinthians 15:1-4 also. A Christian is one who has been spiritually born (regenerated) through faith in the Gospel. He has been cleansed from sin and God indwells his human spirit. Only one who has been born from above is able to learn and utilize spiritual truth and obey God's will. Therefore, an understanding of the new birth and how spirituality works is necessary for some topics contained herein. The book *Answers* details the new birth, and *Bearing Fruit or Living Barren* explains spirituality, both by the authors of *God's Will*.

Man is a spiritual being, and this book makes many references to the operation of spirituality. For example, the terms "inner man," or "inward man," refer to the non-physical mind of man. The terms "spiritual man," "carnal man," and "natural man" describe the condition of the inner man, in accordance with Paul's usage. A Christian who utilizes the power of grace through faith for daily living is known as a spiritual man; he understands and believes God's word, shares God's perspective, and depends upon God's empowerment for the tasks of daily life. His motive comes from the Holy Spirit acting upon his human spirit. A carnal man is a Christian who is operating by the power of his flesh. He is motivated by the principle of sin which operates within his body. He operates this way by choice, living as if he is unsaved. He can immediately return to the condition of spirituality by returning to agreement with God (confession) in regard to his sin. Every Christian is at all times either spiritual or carnal. These are the only two modes of operation possible for a Christian. A natural man is an unsaved man; he is in the natural condition in which he was born, separated from God by sin. A natural man cannot know the things of God nor please God in any way. He is also known as a "soulish man" because the source of his decisions is his soul, the seat of his emotions and will.

We describe a few things differently in our books than what is probably most common. We do so in order to explain functional principles and also to match our explanations to the descriptions found in word-for-word translations of scripture. For example, rather than using the term "sin nature," we use "law of sin," as Paul did, or "sin principle" so that we might remind readers that a law is how something operates (think: law of gravity or Archimedes' principle). In order to distinguish faith from a nebulous mental exercise or wishful thinking, we use the term "faith system." This term serves several purposes. It distinguishes Christian living from Israel's law system. It also contrasts faith to the opposing operating system, the law of sin. It emphasizes that *how* we do God's will is vital, arguably more important than what we do in many cases. It is also a reminder that one is either using faith or one is not. No believer should beat himself up for not having "enough faith;" the adequacy of faith is a function of whether or not a Christian knows the promises of God so that he might have faith in them. Our faith is in *God's* ability, not in our own. We hope that our readers find the language adequately explanatory, helpful, and thought-provoking. Lastly, readers should expect to find some overlap between chapters and subtopics because spirituality is the wellspring of obedience to God and is, therefore, connected to them all.

The King James Version

We, the authors, continue to prefer the King James Version of the Bible and use it primarily. It is free to use, it excels in describing doctrine with precision, and it has centuries of priceless resources keyed to it. We believe it offers a personal benefit as well; the typical reader must slow down and think about what is being read; it is difficult to read one's own thinking and assumptions into a text that is written unlike the way we ordinarily think. In some cases, however, we find its wording to be difficult to decipher for modern readers and have chosen an alternate translation which we believe best represents the meaning of the verse or passage. We hope that those who are King James only in their beliefs recognize that not every verse in the other Bible translations is incorrect.

Quality Over Quantity

…but the Father that dwelleth in me, he doeth the works.
(Jhn 14:10b)

Scripture is loaded with instruction about godly living, describing the attitude and behavior befitting one who is indwelt by God Himself. Because of the Bible's size, it can seem like an overwhelming to-do list. God's teachings in grace, however, are not a to-do list, and we remind readers of this fact throughout the book. God Himself does the work of producing His character within the spiritual man by faith. Things like forgiveness, humility, patience, and joy are the result of spirituality. Therefore, instead of thinking, "I need to do this," we ask our readers to think: "Am I seeing this in myself?" In this way, a Christian can determine if he is functioning by the power of the Spirit. If he does not see the characteristics of spiritual fruit, he can look to the corresponding scriptures and adjust himself to the Spirit by agreeing with God's word. This concept is part of what is known as "the believer's rest." We who are born again are to rest in the complete and sufficient work of Jesus Christ, allowing God to work in and through us by faith. Resting in God's sufficiency to do His work in us is the way in which the truth sets us free from the law, enabling us to obey

God without legal pressure and condemnation. We, the authors, intend to convey that much of God's will addresses the quality and character of Christian living, and that "doing things" is a natural result of an internal change. We hope this book will be a help in facilitating the faith-rest life in those who read it, all to the glory of God.

> *There remaineth therefore a rest to the people of God. For he that is entered into his rest, he also hath ceased from his own works, as God did from his.* (Heb 4:9-10)

CHAPTER 1

GOD WILLS THAT ALL THE WORLD WOULD BE SAVED

... we also believe, and therefore speak... (2 Cor 4:13b)

In eternity past, before anything had been created, God the Father, God the Son, and God the Holy Spirit enjoyed a relationship of perfect love among themselves (Jhn 17:24). Sorrow, pain, and tragedy did not exist. This blissful communion could have continued into eternity future with no dissatisfaction, discontentment, nor lack of anything. The triune God, however, wished to share His quality of life beyond the three persons of the Godhead; God chose to offer the opportunity to know Him and His glorious love to beings that He would create.

> *And I have declared unto them thy name, and will declare it: that the love wherewith thou hast loved me may be in them, and I in them.* (Jhn 17:26)

God created the angelic realm before He created man. The angels began their lives in His presence in heaven, and knowing what they had to lose, many rebelled and departed. No redemption from their choice and its consequences was made available to them (Heb 2:16). God then created man, but as the angels had before, man soon proved that every being who is less than God will behave in a way that is less than godly. Having been given only one law to obey, Adam failed. Now tainted with sin, he was not fit for intimate communion with God. When sin enters into this life, fellowship with a holy God is broken; in the heavenly life to come, sin cannot enter.

But there shall by no means enter it anything that defiles, or causes an abomination or a lie, but only those who are written in the Lamb's Book of Life. (Rev 21:27 NKJV)

Nobody can meet God's holy standards apart from Him; therefore, to sin is to act independently from Him. Adam's decision to exercise independence rather than to trust God resulted in his fall, and through him, the fall of all mankind. Man needed deliverance from the fall and its consequences.

God Made a Way

Knowing that man would fall short of the glory for which he was created, God planned a way of redemption from that fall into sin. A perfect, sinless, substitutionary sacrifice was made by Jesus Christ to pay the debt that humanity owes to God for sinning against Him. Jesus Christ, an infinite person, died on a cross for the infinite sins of the world. He was buried and was raised to life three days later, all in accordance with the scriptures. He was the sin offering on behalf of man, suffering the wrath of God against sin. Every person who, by faith, accepts that payment made on the cross for his sins immediately enters into a secure, everlasting family relationship with God. Jesus Christ, God the Son, took upon Himself humanity; on the cross He bore humanity's sin, and He offers His righteousness to those who believe the Gospel of Christ.

> *For he hath made him* to be *sin for us, who knew no sin; that we might be made the righteousness of God in him.* (2 Cor 5:21)

No person can place any confidence in his own obedience to God; to believe the Gospel is to cast aside all efforts to save oneself and to rely only upon the obedience of the one perfect man who paid sin's penalty according to the will of God.

> *For as by one man's disobedience many were made sinners, so by the obedience of one shall many be made righteous.* (Ro 5:19)

The Holy Spirit Himself seals the believer until that future day of redemption when he leaves this world and enters eternity. This ministry of the Spirit provides a secure and certain future for all who have believed the Gospel for the purpose of salvation from sin.

> *Who hath also sealed us, and given the earnest of the Spirit in our hearts.* (2 Cor 1:22)

> *In whom ye also* trusted, *after that ye heard the word of truth, the gospel of your salvation: in whom also after that ye believed, ye were sealed with that holy Spirit of promise…* (Eph 1:13)

> *And grieve not the holy Spirit of God, whereby ye are sealed unto the day of redemption.* (Eph 4:30)

> *Write ye also for the Jews, as it liketh you, in the king's name, and seal* it *with the king's ring: for the writing which is written in the king's name, and sealed with the king's ring, may no man reverse.* (Est 8:8, see also Dan 6:17 regarding the permanence of a royal seal)

Salvation from sin and its penalty provides eternal life. Eternal life is more than living forever, because everybody lives forever, whether in God's presence or separated from Him. Eternal life is the quality of life that exists in eternity. For man, eternal life results from knowing God:

> *And this is life eternal, that they might know thee the only true God, and Jesus Christ, whom thou hast sent.* (Jhn 17:3)

> *And we know that the Son of God is come, and hath given us an understanding, that we may know him that is true, and we are in him that is true,* even *in his Son Jesus Christ. This is the true God, and eternal life.* (1 Jhn 5:20)

God Has Made Himself Known

> *Abraham saith unto him, They have Moses and the prophets; let them hear them.* (Luk 16:29)

God the Father sent God the Son to provide deliverance from sin, because He desires that all men would be saved from the terrible consequences of sin. These consequences include living as a slave to sin for all of one's earthly life, followed by everlasting separation from God and everlasting punishment. Because of God's desire for man to be saved, He has made His existence known. The proof of God's existence which has been made obvious to mankind is creation, the complexity and delicate balance of which clearly displays the evidence and necessity of a Creator. God did not stop there, however; He also provided man with a conscience. The principles of right and wrong reveal the need for a moral judge, and therefore, the inevitability of judgment to come:

> *For the wrath of God is revealed from heaven against all ungodliness and unrighteousness of men, who hold* (down) *the truth in unrighteousness; Because that which may be known of God is manifest in them; for God hath shewed it unto them. For the invisible things of him from the creation of the world are clearly seen, being understood by the things that are made,* even *his eternal power and Godhead; so that they are without excuse…their conscience also bearing witness, and* their *thoughts the mean while accusing or else excusing one another.* (Ro 1:18-20, 2:15b, clarification added)

God went further to make Himself known to man; He sent prophets, signs, and wonders in order to prove Himself. He went further still, coming to earth in the person of Jesus Christ. Christ's earthly ministry provided innumerable testimonies of God's existence, the coming judgment, and the need for salvation from sin.

> *And beginning at Moses and all the prophets, he expounded unto them in all the scriptures the things concerning himself… And he said unto them, These* are *the words which I spake unto you, while I was yet with you, that all things must be fulfilled, which were written in the law of Moses, and* in *the prophets, and* in *the psalms, concerning me.* (Luk 24:27, 44)

> *This is the disciple which testifieth of these things, and wrote these things: and we know that his testimony is true. And there are also many other things which Jesus did, the which, if they should be written every one, I suppose that even the world itself could not contain the books that should be written. Amen.* (Jhn 21:24-25)

> *To these He also presented Himself alive after His suffering, by many convincing proofs, appearing to them over a period of forty days and speaking of the things concerning the kingdom of God.* (Acts 1:3 NASB)

> *Because he hath appointed a day, in the which he will judge the world in righteousness by that man whom he hath ordained; whereof he hath given assurance unto all men, in that he hath raised him from the dead.* (Acts 17:31)

> *And when they had appointed him a day, there came many to him into his lodging; to whom he expounded and testified the kingdom of God, persuading them concerning Jesus, both out of the law of Moses, and out of the prophets, from morning till evening.* (Acts 28:23)

Finally, God provided a book and preserved it through the centuries so that those who wish to know Him can study it for themselves. The Bible, creation, the conscience, the prophets, the ministry of Jesus, the miracles and signs, and even the miraculous history of Israel itself all testify of the true God who wills that all would be saved.

The Doctrine of Residency

> *(But this spake he of the Spirit, which they that believe on him should receive: for the Holy Ghost was not yet given; because that Jesus was not yet glorified.)* (Jhn 7:39)

God is omnipresent, yet each member of the Godhead has His own role in the universal plan. Throughout history, God's dealings with man have varied in regard to what is being done, where, with whom, and by which divine person. The residency of a member of the Godhead refers to the location of the emphasis of His personal presence and ministry. The doctrine of residency describes the changes in the ministry work of the divine persons; for example, Jesus Christ's residence moved from heaven to earth in order to offer His kingdom to the Nation of Israel. After His death, burial, and resurrection from the dead, He ascended into heaven to the right hand of God the Father to begin a new ministry as an advocate for the saints.

> *My little children, these things write I unto you, that ye sin not. And if any man sin, we have an advocate with the Father, Jesus Christ the righteous.* (1 Jhn 2:1)

Upon Jesus' departure from earth, the Holy Spirit came to earth to begin His new ministries. He became comforter, helper, and illuminator to the saints, and the prosecutor of the lost, convicting them of their sin problem so that they might recognize their need to be saved.

> *But when the Comforter is come, whom I will send unto you from the Father, even the Spirit of truth, which proceedeth from the Father, he shall testify of me*: (Jhn 15:26)

> *Nevertheless I tell you the truth; It is expedient for you that I go away: for if I go not away, the Comforter will not come unto you; but if I depart, I will send him unto you. And when he is come, he will reprove the world of sin, and of righteousness, and of judgment: Of sin, because they believe not on me; Of righteousness, because I go to my Father, and ye see me no more; Of judgment, because the prince of this world is judged.* (Jhn 16:7-11)

The doctrine of residency defines the manner in which God is presently operating and how His people are to partner in ministry with the persons of the Godhead. A change in the residence of a divine person and its accompanying events draw attention to God's purpose and message. Understanding what God is doing today is necessary for Christians to operate in accordance with His will. The residency of God is yet another way that He brings unto Himself all who will come.

God Brings About His Will for the World Through the Agency of the Church

> *But watch thou in all things, endure afflictions, do the work of an evangelist, make full proof of thy ministry.* (2 Tim 4:5)

God provided several ways by which man can know that He exists. The witness of creation, the witness of each man's conscience, and the ministry of Jesus Christ all testify to the reality of the God of the Bible. Many of those who believe in God will, however, spend eternity in the lake of fire. A general belief in God does not provide salvation from sin's penalty. Together with the convicting work of the Holy Spirit, the members of the body of Christ are God's agents to spread the good news of salvation.

> *Give none offence, neither to the Jews, nor to the Gentiles, nor to the church of God: Even as I please all men in all things, not seeking mine own profit, but the profit of many, that they may be saved.* (1 Cor 10:32-33)

> *And of some have compassion, making a difference: And others save with fear, pulling them out of the fire; hating even the garment spotted by the flesh.* (Jude 1:22-23)

The Gospel is the Power of God unto Salvation (Ro 1:16)

> *…that the Gentiles by my mouth should hear the word of the gospel, and believe.* (Acts 15:7b)

Jesus saves. How? By faith. Faith in what? By faith in the message of the Gospel of Christ, 1 Corinthians 15:1-4, which declares the object of faith for salvation; it plainly states what Jesus Christ did to save mankind so that any man might accept Jesus' payment for his sins. Because of the payment He made on the cross for sins, it is not sin, per se, that stands between God and the unsaved man, but unbelief of the truth concerning the Gospel, which asks him to believe that his sin debt was fully paid by Christ's substitutionary sacrifice. God provided a way for man to know Him and to be saved, but each person must believe and accept it rather than reject it.

> *For after that in the wisdom of God the world by wisdom knew not God, it pleased God by the foolishness of preaching to save them that believe.* (1 Cor 1:21)

> *… for in Christ Jesus I have begotten you through the gospel.* (1 Cor 4:15b)

> *That the Gentiles should be fellowheirs, and of the same body, and partakers of his promise in Christ by the gospel…* (Eph 3:6)

> *Who hath saved us, and called* us *with an holy calling, not according to our works, but according to his own purpose and grace, which was given us in Christ Jesus before the world began, But is now made manifest by the appearing of our Saviour Jesus Christ, who hath abolished death, and hath brought life and immortality to light through the gospel…* (2 Tim 1:9-10)

> *Being born again, not of corruptible seed, but of incorruptible, by the word of God...* (1 Pet 1:23a)

Each Christian who desires to cooperate with God in His work will endeavor to spread the Gospel of Christ so that others might be saved. The message that the saints are to share and explain is this:

> *Moreover, brethren, I declare unto you the gospel which I preached unto you, which also ye have received, and wherein ye stand; By which also ye are saved, if ye keep in memory what I preached unto you, unless ye have believed in vain. For I delivered unto you first of all that which I also received, how that Christ died for our sins according to the scriptures; And that he was buried, and that he rose again the third day according to the scriptures...* (1 Cor 15:1-4)

The context of the Gospel includes evidence in the form of hundreds of witnesses to the resurrected Christ:

> *And that he was seen of Cephas, then of the twelve: After that, he was seen of above five hundred brethren at once; of whom the greater part remain unto this present, but some are fallen asleep. After that, he was seen of James; then of all the apostles. And last of all he was seen of me also, as of one born out of due time.* (1 Cor 15:5-8)

God did all these things because His abiding will for man is that he might forever enjoy the blessings of His love and grace. Because of the ravages of sin, man cannot yet experience every aspect of it fully, but God made a way for any who will to enter a perfect world in the future. Not every person will believe and accept salvation. Not every person will even acknowledge God, but that fact reflects no shortcoming on God's part. God is glorified in every person who recognizes His good grace and is saved. In regard to those who refuse His offer, God is glorified in His perfect justice.

Jesus answered and said unto them, This is the work of God, that ye believe on him whom he hath sent. (Jhn 6:29)

For God so loved the world, that he gave his only begotten Son, that whosoever believeth in him should not perish, but have everlasting life. For God sent not his Son into the world to condemn the world; but that the world through him might be saved. He that believeth on him is not condemned: but he that believeth not is condemned already, because he hath not believed in the name of the only begotten Son of God. And this is the condemnation, that light is come into the world, and men loved darkness rather than light, because their deeds were evil. (Jhn 3:16-19)

For this is *good and acceptable in the sight of God our Saviour; Who will have all men to be saved, and to come unto the knowledge of the truth. For* there is *one God, and one mediator between God and men, the man Christ Jesus; Who gave himself a ransom for all, to be testified in due time.* (1 Tim 2:3-6)

The Lord is not slack concerning his promise, as some men count slackness; but is longsuffering to us-ward, not willing that any should perish, but that all should come to repentance. (2 Pet 3:9)

CHAPTER 2

GOD WILLS THAT CHRISTIANS KNOW HIM THROUGH HIS WORD

Even the Spirit of truth; whom the world cannot receive, because it seeth him not, neither knoweth him: but ye know him; for he dwelleth with you, and shall be in you. (Jhn 14:17)

From the first verse of Genesis through the last verse of The Revelation, Jesus Christ is there. The Bible is the story of the Creator, Israel's Messiah, Immanuel—God with us, the incarnate Word of God who has communicated the will of God to man.

> *Search the scriptures; for in them ye think ye have eternal life: and they are they which testify of me.* (Jhn 5:39)
>
> *In the beginning God created the heaven and the earth.* (Gen 1:1)
>
> *In the beginning was the Word, and the Word was with God, and the Word was God. The same was in the beginning with God. All things were made by him; and without him was not any thing made that was made.* (Jhn 1:1-3)
>
> *He which testifieth these things saith, Surely I come quickly. Amen. Even so, come, Lord Jesus. The grace of our Lord Jesus Christ be with you all. Amen.* (Rev 22:20-21)

The first prophecy of the Messiah (savior) is found in Genesis 3:15; His story unfolds throughout the Old Testament which records Israel's heritage, history, and future. During Christ's earthly ministry to Israel, He taught the constitution of the coming kingdom, offering that kingdom to the elect nation, the one chosen to do His work (Ex 19:5-6, Is 43:10, Mt 10:5-7). In anticipation of His rejection by Israel, Jesus reveals the coming of the Holy Spirit in a new ministry (Jhn 17). After His resurrection, Christ teaches Paul the mysteries of the church and the operation of the grace-through-faith program; the faith system of Christ is now taught to Spirit-filled Christians when they read the epistles, the letters which were written to the church.

> *How that by revelation he made known unto me the mystery* (now revealed); *(as I wrote afore in few words, Whereby, when ye **read**, ye may understand my knowledge in the mystery of Christ)* (Eph 3:3-4, clarification added)

> Even *the mystery which hath been hid from ages and from generations, but now is made manifest to his saints: To whom God would make known what is the riches of the glory of this mystery among the Gentiles; which is Christ in you, the hope* (expectation) *of glory* (right now): (Col 1:26-27, clarification added)

> *That their hearts might be comforted, being knit together in love, and unto all riches of the full assurance of understanding, to the acknowledgement of the mystery of God, and of the Father, and of Christ; In whom are hid all the treasures of wisdom and knowledge.* (Col 2:2-3)

It is a benefit beyond measure to learn that which God has revealed about Himself. What more valuable enterprise could there be than to search the Bible for its treasures, knowing for oneself the very word of the one true God? His written word teaches everything God desires man to know of Him and His will, promising that those who are born again can understand it. It is the sacred privilege and duty of each believer to study the Bible, to teach it to other Christians and to children, and to proclaim the Gospel of Christ to non-Christians. No person can claim to be doing God's will if he does not know God's word, for it is the only place in which His will can be found.

> *Now we have received, not the spirit of the world, but the spirit which is of God; that we might know the things that are freely given to us of God… For who hath known the mind of the Lord, that he may instruct him? But we have the mind of Christ.* (1 Cor 2:12, 16)

> *That the God of our Lord Jesus Christ, the Father of glory, may give unto you the spirit of wisdom and revelation in the knowledge of him…* (Eph 1:17)

> *And this I pray, that your love may abound yet more and more in knowledge and in all judgment; That ye may approve things that are excellent; that ye may be sincere and without offence till the day of Christ…* (Phil 1:9-10)

> *For this cause we also, since the day we heard it, do not cease to pray for you, and to desire that ye might be filled with the knowledge of his will in all wisdom and spiritual understanding…* (Col 1:9)

> *Study to shew thyself approved unto God, a workman that needeth not to be ashamed, rightly dividing the word of truth.* (2 Tim 2:15)
>
> *But continue thou in the things which thou hast learned and hast been assured of...* (2 Tim 3:14a)
>
> *Grace and peace be multiplied unto you through the knowledge of God, and of Jesus our Lord...* (2 Pet 1:2)
>
> *According as his divine power hath given unto us all things that* pertain *unto life and godliness, through the knowledge of him that hath called us to glory and virtue...* (2 Pet 1:3)

God Provides

> *But the Comforter,* which is *the Holy Ghost, whom the Father will send in my name, he shall teach you all things, and bring all things to your remembrance, whatsoever I have said unto you.* (Jhn 14:26)

God wills that His children know Him through His word, and no Christian need fear that he cannot because the Bible is beyond his capability. Cooperation with God does not depend upon one's educational level or intellectual ability. God has already taken the varying abilities of individuals into account. He is able to bypass shortcomings, and to that end He sent the Holy Spirit to be the believer's helper. The Spirit illuminates and teaches the mind of the spiritual man to understand and apply God's word. Using the non-physical human spirit, God brings to remembrance those truths from His word which are needed for the daily guidance of the spiritual man. The more that he learns from God's word, the more that is available for God to minister to him.

> *But God hath revealed* them *unto us by his Spirit: for the Spirit searcheth all things, yea, the deep things of God. For what man knoweth the things of a man, save the spirit of man which is in him? even so the things of God knoweth no man, but the Spirit of God. Now we have received, not the spirit of the world, but the spirit which is of God; that we might know the things that are freely given to us of God. Which things also we speak, not in the words which man's wisdom teacheth, but which the Holy Ghost teacheth; comparing spiritual things with spiritual. But the natural man receiveth not the things of the Spirit of God: for they are foolishness unto him: neither can he know* them, *because they are spiritually discerned.* (1 Cor 2:10-14)

> *But these things have I told you, that when the time shall come, ye may remember that I told you of them.* (Jhn 16:4a)

> *Howbeit when he, the Spirit of truth, is come, he will guide you into all truth: for he shall not speak of himself; but whatsoever he shall hear,* that *shall he speak: and he will shew you things to come.* (Jhn 16:13)

> *That the God of our Lord Jesus Christ, the Father of glory, may give unto you the spirit of wisdom and revelation in the knowledge of him: The eyes of your understanding being enlightened; that ye may know what is the hope of his calling, and what the riches of the glory of his inheritance in the saints…* (Eph 1:17-18)

> *Wherefore be ye not unwise, but understanding what the will of the Lord is.* (Eph 5:17)
>
> *Let us therefore, as many as be perfect, be thus minded: and if in any thing ye be otherwise minded, God shall reveal even this unto you.* (Phil 3:15)
>
> *Consider what I say; and the Lord give thee understanding in all things.* (2 Tim 2:7)

In addition to the personal blessing of knowing God, the saint blesses others when he knows scripture well enough to explain and teach it. Doing so is the normal expectation for every Christian (Heb 5:12). Pastors, teachers, and mature believers are all part of God's plan to enable understanding and remembrance, the purposes of which include helping new believers to mature and enabling all members to carry out the work of the ministry.

> *For this cause have I sent unto you Timotheus, who is my beloved son, and faithful in the Lord, who shall bring you into remembrance of my ways which be in Christ, as I teach every where in every church.* (1 Cor 4:17)
>
> *Wherefore I will not be negligent to put you always in remembrance of these things, though ye know* them, *and be established in the present truth. Yea, I think it meet, as long as I am in this tabernacle, to stir you up by putting you in remembrance; ... Moreover I will endeavor that ye may be able after my decease to have these things always in remembrance.* (2 Pet 1:12-13, 15)

> *This second epistle, beloved, I now write unto you; in both which I stir up your pure minds by way of remembrance: That ye may be mindful of the words which were spoken before by the holy prophets, and of the commandment of us the apostles of the Lord and Saviour...* (2 Pet 3:1-2)

> *And the things that thou hast heard of me among many witnesses, the same commit thou to faithful men, who shall be able to teach others also.* (2 Tim 2:2)

> *And the servant of the Lord must not strive; but be gentle unto all men, apt to teach, patient...* (2 Tim 2:24)

> *The aged women likewise, that they be in behaviour as becometh holiness, not false accusers, not given to much wine, teachers of good things; That they may teach the young women to be sober, to love their husbands, to love their children...* (Titus 2:3-4)

> *And he gave some, apostles; and some, prophets; and some, evangelists; and some, pastors and teachers; For the perfecting of the saints, for the work of the ministry, for the edifying of the body of Christ...* (Eph 4:11-12; The early church was given a variety of teachers to equip the saints. Apostles and prophets laid the foundation. Teachers of evangelism and shepherding teachers—pastors—continued the work of the ministry.)

The Bible states that it contains *all* things needed for life and godliness, and that it thoroughly furnishes the Christian unto all good works. This means that when a believer is illuminated to doctrine from scripture, he can immediately begin to apply it to his life and ministry.

> *All scripture is given by inspiration of God, and is profitable for doctrine* (things which are to be known and believed but are not practiced; Genesis, or the Law of Moses, for example), *for reproof, for correction, for instruction in righteousness* (three uses for those doctrines which are to be both believed and practiced)*: That the man of God may be perfect, throughly furnished unto all good works.* (2 Tim 3:16-17, clarification added)

As a practical matter, not every Christian agrees upon the meaning of every doctrine. Can the body of Christ obey God if its members cannot determine His instructions? The matter of practical unity will be addressed further in Chapter 8, but for the purposes of this chapter, the solution to varying levels of understanding is to have spiritual meekness (teachability) and faith in God's promises. Since God says His word can be understood, then it can be; the many verses listed previously confirm this. "Agree to disagree" is not found in biblical examples; instead, Christians are called to search and study the scriptures. Not every Christian is illuminated to the same degree, but each should at least be willing to continue learning, to be taught, and even to be corrected in order to avoid harming the body of Christ with erroneous teaching. If the fervent desire of every Christian heart was for God to teach him the truth and to reveal his ignorance and error, the church could once again "turn the world upside down," (Acts 17:6). The Christian who opens a word-for-word translation of the Bible daily and asks God to illuminate both his misunderstandings and the truth will be granted his request.

The Christian Obligation to God's Word

> *Hold fast the form of sound* (healthy, appropriately applied) *words, which thou hast heard of me, in faith and love which is in Christ Jesus.* (2 Tim 1:13, clarification added)

The born-again Christian is in a relationship with Almighty God, but no relationship can flourish if one member believes falsities about the other. Knowing God means knowing the truth about Him, and no person can know God apart from His own revelation of Himself and His program. Knowledge and understanding of grace doctrine is vital to the spiritual health of individual church members, the congregation as a whole, and to the Christian faith itself. Therefore, the church has a duty to protect it. Christians must stand boldly against erroneous teaching whether it is intentional or unintentional. There is no fellowship apart from the truth, and incorrect teaching is as powerless as ignorance. It is also harmful. Satan, the deceiver, wants to cause misunderstanding, misuse, and division so that Christ's body cannot fulfill its calling to share the good news of salvation.

> *As I urged you upon my departure for Macedonia, remain on at Ephesus so that you may instruct certain men not to teach strange doctrines, nor to pay attention to myths and endless genealogies, which give rise to mere speculation rather than furthering* the administration of God which is by faith. *... For some men, straying from these things, have turned aside to fruitless discussion, wanting to be teachers of the Law, even though they do not understand either what they are saying or the matters about which they make confident assertions.* (1 Tim 1:3-4, 6-7 NASB)

> *If thou put the brethren in remembrance of these things, thou shalt be a good minister of Jesus Christ, nourished up in the words of faith and of good doctrine, whereunto thou hast attained. But refuse profane and old wives' fables, and exercise thyself rather unto godliness.* (1 Tim 4:6-7)
>
> *Till I come, give attendance to reading, to exhortation, to doctrine...Meditate upon these things; give thyself wholly to them; that thy profiting may appear to all. Take heed unto thyself, and unto the doctrine; continue in them: for in doing this thou shalt both save thyself* (from your spiritual enemies), *and them that hear thee* (from being misled by you). (1 Tim 4:13, 15-16, clarification added)

False Teaching Undermines Obedience to God's Will

> *And Jesus answering said unto them, Do ye not therefore err, because ye know not the scriptures, neither the power of God?* (Mark 12:24, see also Matt 22:29)

God conveyed His will to Israel through the prophets and priests. Warnings about false prophets are found throughout the Bible; they could be recognized when a prophecy failed. Church doctrine was given to the Apostles and New Testament prophets and spread by letters (epistles) which were verified, copied, and widely circulated (Eph 2:20, 3:5; 1 Cor 3:10; Gal 1:11-12, 18, 2:2; Acts 15:23, 16:4-5). Upon the completion of the canon of scripture, those who claimed to be prophets were known to be liars; the new problem for the church became false teachers.

> *But there **were false prophets** also among the people, even as there **shall be false teachers** among you, who privily shall bring in damnable heresies, even denying the Lord that bought them, and bring upon themselves swift destruction.* (2 Pet 2:1)

> *O Timothy, keep that which is committed to thy trust, avoiding profane* and *vain babblings, and oppositions of science falsely so called: Which some professing have erred concerning the faith.* (1 Tim 6:20-21a)

> *Preach the word; be instant in season, out of season; reprove, rebuke, exhort with all longsuffering and doctrine. For the time will come when they will not endure sound doctrine; but after their own lusts shall they heap to themselves teachers, having itching ears; And they shall turn away* their *ears from the truth, and shall be turned unto fables.* (2 Tim 4:2-4)

> *Beloved, when I gave all diligence to write unto you of the common salvation, it was needful for me to write unto you, and exhort* you *that ye should earnestly contend for the faith which was **once** delivered unto the saints.* (Jude 1:3)

The Apostles expected their readers to know scripture well enough that they would recognize false teaching. Having recognized it, they were not to have anything whatsoever to do with someone who denied, misapplied, or misrepresented God's word and refused correction. They were not to do so much as offer good wishes to one who would corrupt God's precious communication to man. It was not considered "loving" to allow false teaching to go unchallenged, and this expectation of God has not been rescinded. God's will regarding error is not ambiguous.

Whosoever transgresseth, and abideth not in the doctrine of Christ, hath not God. He that abideth in the doctrine of Christ, he hath both the Father and the Son. If there come any unto you, and bring not this doctrine, receive him not into your house, neither bid him God speed… (2 Jhn 1:9-10)

Now I beseech you, brethren, mark them which cause divisions and offences contrary to the doctrine which ye have learned; and avoid them. For they that are such serve not our Lord Jesus Christ, but their own belly; and by good words and fair speeches deceive the hearts of the simple. (Ro 16:17-18)

I marvel that ye are so soon removed from him that called you into the grace of Christ unto another gospel: Which is not another; but there be some that trouble you, and would pervert the gospel of Christ. But though we, or an angel from heaven, preach any other gospel unto you than that which we have preached unto you, let him be accursed. As we said before, so say I now again, If any man *preach any other gospel unto you than that ye have received, let him be accursed.* (Gal 1:6-9)

Let as many servants as are under the yoke count their own masters worthy of all honour, that the name of God and his *doctrine be not blasphemed… If any man teach otherwise, and consent not to wholesome words,* even *the words of our Lord Jesus Christ, and to the doctrine which is according to godliness…from such withdraw thyself.* (1 Tim 6:1, 3, 5b)

Do not err, my beloved brethren. (Jas 1:16)

The epistles to the church contain many strong warnings about the danger of false teaching. Protecting the integrity of grace doctrine is so important that there is a special warning to those who are responsible for teaching others.

> *My brethren, be not many masters* (teachers), *knowing that we shall receive the greater condemnation.* (Ja 3:1, synonym added)

Only integrity in the teaching of God's word effectively transmits the saving message to those outside the church and offers the spiritual food for maturity to those within. Every Christian needs to understand God's word in order to do God's will and avoid falling into error. Erroneous teaching will ultimately lead to personal sin and will also spread, thereby adversely affecting others.

Failing to understand God's offer of grace through faith alone has terrible, everlasting consequences for the unsaved; the ability to transmit it correctly, explain it thoroughly, and answer questions about it is essential. Although the saints' redemption is secured with the blood of Christ, there are serious consequences for scriptural ignorance and deception. One's entire earthly life can be wasted, dishonoring the Lord and making useless the life of service and victory that He died to provide. There is a reason that tears will be wiped away in heaven; many will be deeply grieved for casting aside the many opportunities they had to bless others with the knowledge of their precious Savior.

Take heed therefore unto yourselves, and to all the flock, over the which the Holy Ghost hath made you overseers, to feed the church of God, which he hath purchased with his own blood. For I know this, that after my departing shall grievous wolves enter in among you, not sparing the flock. Also of your own selves shall men arise, speaking perverse things, to draw away disciples after them. Therefore watch, and remember, that by the space of three years I ceased not to warn every one night and day with tears. And now, brethren, I commend you to God, and to the word of his grace, which is able to build you up, and to give you an inheritance among all them which are sanctified. (Acts 20:28-32)

But I fear, lest by any means, as the serpent beguiled Eve through his subtilty, so your minds should be corrupted from the simplicity that is in Christ. (2 Cor 11:3)

That we henceforth *be no more children, tossed to and fro, and carried about with every wind of doctrine, by the sleight of men,* and *cunning craftiness, whereby they lie in wait to deceive...* (Eph 4:14)

And this I say, lest any man should beguile you with enticing words... Beware lest any man spoil you through philosophy and vain deceit, after the tradition of men, after the rudiments of the world, and not after Christ. (Col 2:4, 8)

But evil men and seducers shall wax worse and worse, deceiving, and being deceived. But continue thou in the things which thou hast learned and hast been assured of, knowing of whom thou hast learned them... (2 Tim 3:13-14)

For there are certain men crept in unawares, who were before of old ordained to this condemnation, ungodly men, turning the grace of our God into lasciviousness, and denying the only Lord God, and our Lord Jesus Christ. (Jude 1:4)

A Christian who neglects Bible reading and study must not allow himself to believe that he is fulfilling God's will. Without careful study and thorough understanding of God's word, one cannot apply it to the daily events, opportunities, thoughts, and reactions of everyday life. Christians need not worry about not being up to the task of Christian living. Everything God asks of His children He also enables them to do.

These things command and teach. (1 Tim 4:11)

There is value in regularly taking an honest evaluation of oneself by asking things such as, "Do I really want to know God in a way that impacts daily life? Do I believe that His way of living is best? What do I want for eternity? Are the rewards He offers more or less important to me than doing what I want in the here and now?" God wants His children to know Him, to work closely with Him, and to operate as spiritual men for His glory. To glorify God is to promote a good opinion of Him. He is glorified when Christians implement grace teaching by faith, thereby displaying God's character and acting accordingly.

The Bible is a big book. It is not easily read nor rapidly comprehended. To know God and do His will, the Christian must decide whether or not he truly wishes for the Lord to be first in all things. If the answer is yes, he must do the work of learning His word and His ways; no Christian will ever regret that decision.

God's Will

Now the God of peace, that brought again from the dead our Lord Jesus, that great shepherd of the sheep, through the blood of the everlasting covenant, Make you perfect in every good work to do his will, working in you that which is wellpleasing in his sight, through Jesus Christ; to whom be glory for ever and ever. Amen. (Heb 13:20-21)

CHAPTER 3

GOD WILLS THAT CHRISTIANS ADOPT THE DIVINE VIEWPOINT

Can two walk together, except they be agreed? (Amos 3:3)

The God of the Bible is love. He has good intentions for man and has made it known through His book, the Bible. God graciously provided the church with this written record of His will so that those who wish to can cooperate in carrying out His current program. The partnership that God offers man is known as fellowship, a relationship which requires agreement and common understanding. To operate according to God's will, a Christian's view of the world, of experiences, and of himself and others must be in accordance with the view which God Himself has of these things.

God Wills That Christians View Themselves Correctly

Not that we are sufficient of ourselves to think any thing as of ourselves; but our sufficiency is of God…
(2 Cor 3:5)

A Christian's spiritual birth is the beginning of a relationship with God (Jhn 3:7). In relationships, a person's willingness to be honest with himself is vital. A person who is unwilling to examine his attitudes, motives, behaviors, desires, assumptions, and expectations will often find himself at odds with others. A Christian who desires to cooperate with God must be willing to examine himself, allowing himself to be critiqued and changed by the purifying truths of scripture (Heb 4:12). As the truth transforms the believer, he finds himself doing things that are uncomfortable, forsaking things that are worthless, and treating people better than they might seem to deserve. By recognizing that everything he has was given to him by God, the spiritual man can ignore outward differences and societal distinctions and put others first (Col 3:10-11). His sacrificial mindset helps him avoid pride regarding his qualities and abilities. He knows that God the Son did not die to save him because he deserved it; he was saved in spite of what he deserved. He knows that in order to fulfill God's will he must continually renew his mind with the divine viewpoint and agree with God (2 Cor 4:16, Eph 4:23). A correct view of humanity in general, and of himself in particular, motivates him to selflessly evangelize the lost and serve the body of Christ.

> *Now these things, brethren, I have figuratively applied to myself and Apollos for your sakes, so that in us you may learn not to exceed what is written, so that no one of you will become arrogant in behalf of one against the other. For who regards you as superior? What do you have that you did not receive? And if you did receive it, why do you boast as if you had not received it?* (1 Cor 4:6-7 NASB)

> *And that he died for all, that they which live should not henceforth live unto themselves, but unto him which died for them, and rose again.* (2 Cor 5:15)

> *And be not conformed to this world: but be ye transformed by the renewing of your mind, that ye may prove what is that good, and acceptable, and perfect, will of God. For I say, through the grace given unto me, to every man that is among you, not to think of himself more highly than he ought to think…Be of the same mind one toward another. Mind not high things, but condescend to men of low estate. Be not wise in your own conceits.* (Ro 12:2, 3a, 16)

> *Let this mind be in you, which was also in Christ Jesus: Who, being in the form of God, thought it not robbery to be equal with God: But made himself of no reputation, and took upon him the form of a servant, and was made in the likeness of men: And being found in fashion as a man, he humbled himself, and became obedient unto death, even the death of the cross.* (Phil 2:5-8)

Man naturally seeks his own will and his own way. Though he might deny it and appear to do the opposite, he actively loves himself: he does what he likes and what feels good to him. Even those who engage in destructive behaviors are practicing a form of self-love; such a person does what he wants to do regardless of the potential for negative consequences. The enjoyment he finds in a risky or harmful experience is greater than the fear or dislike of the result. The Bible flatly denies today's explanations, diagnoses, and claims which assert that man does not love himself.

> *For **no man ever** yet hated his own flesh; but nourisheth and cherisheth it…* (Eph 5:29)

To think rightly of oneself is to avoid both the extremes of self-pitying put-downs and high-mindedness. Self-righteous pride is often easy to recognize, but complaints about oneself are a form of pride also, revealing an attitude of entitlement and covetousness for something better, whether it is beauty, a better physique, more talent, or a superior brain. To put oneself down is an expression of contempt for what God provided and a denial that one is "fearfully and wonderfully made;" it is a complaint against God. Thankfulness to God without pride or denigration should be the attitude toward all that one is and has. God calls any other mindset a foolish deception which will lead to the downfall of a Christian.

For if a man think himself to be something, when he is nothing, he deceiveth himself. (Gal 6:3)

Let no man deceive himself. If any man among you seemeth to be wise in this world, let him become a fool, that he may be wise. (1 Cor 3:18)

Wherefore let him that thinketh he standeth take heed lest he fall. (1 Cor 10:12)

For we dare not make ourselves of the number, or compare ourselves with some that commend themselves: but they measuring themselves by themselves, and comparing themselves among themselves, are not wise. (2 Cor 10:12)

A Godly Motive is Part of the Divine Viewpoint

And whatsoever ye do in word or deed, do all in the name of the Lord Jesus, giving thanks to God and the Father by him. (Col 3:17)

A correct view of oneself begins at salvation when a person recognizes his wretched sinfulness and acknowledges his need for a savior. As a Christian matures, it becomes obvious to him that he must know spiritual things and not simply do things. As he sees that he must depend upon God in all that he does, his internal condition must be taken into account. Mere external compliance does not satisfy God's righteousness. A "good deed" done with a poor attitude or a selfish motive has no spiritual value and does not fool Him. The quality of the work is as important as what is being done, and any work produced by the flesh is counted to be of the same quality as sin (Ro 14:23). A Christian who does good works out of obligation or because of pressure is not utilizing the faith system and is therefore operating by the principle (law) of sin.

> *Where* is *boasting then? It is excluded. By what law? of works? Nay: but by the law* (operating principle) *of faith.* (Ro 3:27, clarification added)
>
> *The sting of death* is *sin; and the strength of sin* is *the law.* (1 Cor 15:56, Any external law can shift operation away from the internal way of operating by faith. Christians are to obey laws by faith, meaning they trust God to enable them to obey.)

God does not expect nor want Christians to dredge up a "positive attitude" from the mire of the sin-tainted soul. The power of the grace-through-faith system renews the mind (spirit and soul) using spiritual truth, thereby enabling cooperation motivated by God's love working within him. The spiritual man pauses throughout his day, using those truths to evaluate himself and allowing God's love and grace to refresh his attitude. The products of a pure motive and a glad heart bring glory to God. By evaluating his inner man, a Christian can align himself with God's will and produce spiritual fruit and good works by faith, adjusting himself as necessary when his attitude begins to slip or his motive becomes selfish.

Ye ask, and receive not, because ye ask amiss, that ye may consume it upon your lusts. (Ja 4:3)

And let ours also learn to maintain good works for necessary uses, that they be not unfruitful. (Titus 3:14)

Motive matters even in "necessary uses," such as things that must be done routinely as part of daily living. Mowing the lawn, cooking dinner, cleaning, and occupational duties are all to be done "as to the Lord." When mundane chores are done with gratitude and contentment, they become good works, and the time spent on them is not unfruitful. The Christian who does ordinary things with a right mindset produces the fruit of the Spirit by faith, which glorifies God. God knows that the saints must earn a living, take care of their homes and families, and do many other tasks to maintain earthly lives. He has not created a system in which a busy parent or an employee who works overtime cannot earn heavenly rewards and bring Him glory. The spiritual man can live unto God in all that he does. Conversely, without accessing the power of grace through faith, the Christian does not please God, even if he is doing an impressive religious activity. Each Christian must determine for himself whether or not his motive is to serve God. If it is, God then fills him with the desire and strength to do so.

For it is God which worketh in you both to will and to do of his good pleasure. (Phil 2:13)

> *Ye are bought with a price; be not ye the servants of men.* (1 Cor 7:23)

> *Not with eyeservice, as menpleasers; but as the servants of Christ, doing the will of God from the heart* (literally the soul, the seat of volition); *With good will doing service, as to the Lord, and not to men…* (Eph 6:6-7, clarification added)

> *And whatsoever ye do, do* it *heartily* (from the soul), *as to the Lord, and not unto men…* (Col 3:23, literal translation added)

> *Not slothful in business; fervent in spirit; serving the Lord…* (Ro 12:11)

> *So then they that are in the flesh cannot please God.* (Ro 8:8)

> *But without faith* it is *impossible to please* him… (Heb 11:6a)

> *Furthermore then we beseech you, brethren, and exhort* you *by the Lord Jesus, that as ye have received of us how ye ought to walk and to please God, so ye would abound more and more.* (1 Thes 4:1)

Paul's teaching regarding the mind of Christ (1 Cor 2:16) is realized when the Christian determines to please the Father and adopts the divine viewpoint.

> *And he that sent me is with me: the Father hath not left me alone; for I do always those things that please him.* (Jhn 8:29)

The Christian life is a spiritual life; it is the outworking of God's character through knowing God and understanding the principles of grace. Grace truths are meant to inform the beliefs, attitudes, and opinions of the spiritual man so he might produce works which are of an acceptable quality, produced by God Himself through faith. The spiritual man knows what God has promised, and believes that God will produce His character within him. He believes that God will enable him to do what the scripture teaches, and He does. The current program of administering believers by grace emphasizes the condition and contents of the Christian mind, which in turn produces spiritual fruit from the inside out. Whereas the Law of Moses set external limits on man that he could not keep, the spiritual man's motives are aligned with the divine viewpoint, resulting in a desire to live accordingly and the power to do so.

God Wills That Christians Control Their Thoughts

> We are *destroying speculations and every lofty thing raised up against the knowledge of God, and* we are *taking every thought captive to the obedience of Christ...*
> (2 Cor 10:5 NASB)

Part of sharing God's viewpoint includes avoiding those things which would lead one away from spirituality and into carnality. Knowing and believing God and His word facilitates spiritual living, but due to the power and ubiquity of modern messaging, a godly view of self, of others, and of the world is not easy to maintain. There is an intense battle to influence, deceive, and defile the Christian mind. It is God's will that each Christian protects his mind, which is to be aligned with the divine viewpoint in all matters. In order to do so, the Christian must control his thought life.

When a Christian is spiritual, his realistic view of himself keeps him open to correction. When grace doctrine is read or taught, the Holy Spirit brings to mind those things in his physical life and his thought life which contradict it so that the spiritual man might adjust himself and maintain his spiritual condition. Protecting one's mind includes renewing one's mind with grace teaching, as well as actively limiting one's thinking to things which are godly and good. Examples include refusing to fret or ruminate upon disappointment, self-pity, anger, the unchangeable past, the sins of others, things wished for, and temptations to sin. It is not a "Pollyanna" mindset or ignoring reality to focus on the good; it is the way in which God directs the believer to avoid Satanic mental traps. Every person has the ability to control his own mind, and the Christian has both a mandate and a supernatural empowerment to do so. The spiritual Christian rests in the peacefulness of an unruffled mind because he trusts completely in God.

> *Set your mind on the things above, not on the things that are on earth.* (Col 3:2 NASB)

> *Finally, brethren, whatsoever things are true, whatsoever things* are *honest, whatsoever things* are *just, whatsoever things* are *pure, whatsoever things* are *lovely, whatsoever things* are *of good report; if* there be *any virtue, and if* there be *any praise, think on these things.* (Phil 4:8)

> *While we look not at the things which are seen, but at the things which are not seen: for the things which are seen* are *temporal; but the things which are not seen* are *eternal.* (2 Cor 4:18)

> *And the peace of God, which passeth all understanding, shall keep your hearts and minds through Christ Jesus.* (Phil 4:7)
>
> *Brethren, I count not myself to have apprehended: but this one thing I do, forgetting those things which are behind, and reaching forth unto those things which are before, I press toward the mark for the prize of the high calling of God in Christ Jesus. Let us therefore, as many as be perfect, be thus minded:* ***and if in any thing ye be otherwise minded****, God shall reveal even this unto you.* (Phil 3:13-15)
>
> *That ye be not soon shaken in mind, or be troubled...*
> (2 Thes 2:2a)

The non-physical spirit and soul comprise the inward (inner) man, also known as the mind. Spirituality is so utterly foreign to the human mind that renewing it with the truth of God's word is something that a Christian must do all of his life. Furthermore, the mind is continually under attack from the three enemies with Satanically-inspired false teaching, worldly philosophy, and fleshly filth. In addition to studying the word at church services and other gatherings, a Christian can read, speak, and sing to himself in order to reinforce grace doctrine; doing so will protect his mind, and facilitate mental control and emotional stability. Bible teaching, scripture reading, memorization, and doctrinally accurate song all facilitate the renewing of the mind and the wise application of truth.

> *Speaking to yourselves in psalms and hymns and spiritual songs, singing and making melody in your heart to the Lord...*
> (Eph 5:19)

> *Let the word of Christ dwell in you richly in all wisdom; teaching and admonishing one another in psalms and hymns and spiritual songs, singing with grace in your hearts to the Lord.* (Col 3:16)

> *And be not conformed to this world: but be ye transformed by the renewing of your mind, that ye may prove what is that good, and acceptable, and perfect, will of God.* (Ro 12:2)

> *And be renewed in the spirit of your mind…* (Eph 4:23)

> *For which cause we faint not; but though our outward man perish, yet the inward man is renewed day by day.* (2 Cor 4:16)

> *That he would grant you, according to the riches of his glory, to be strengthened with might by his Spirit in the inner man…* (Eph 3:16)

It is the will of God that His children live a life of purity, avoiding the pollutions of this world's philosophies and methods. Purity in conduct must begin with purity of mind. That which comes from the mind of God is pure, and as the spiritual man limits his mind to the truths from above and to good and decent things, it has a purifying effect. The Christian who keeps his mind from running wild protects himself from the attitudes and persuasions which lead to trouble and sin.

Does this mean that he cannot think about his job, family, or pursuits he enjoys? No; limiting one's mind for the sake of purity is not legalism or some impossible standard. It means that the spiritual man regularly evaluates his thought-life and attitude.

The mind of Christ cannot co-exist with a fleshly mind. Therefore, when ungodly thoughts are recognized, the spiritual man returns to agreement with God. He might take a moment to say to himself, "I have the mind of Christ; I do not need to allow myself to think about this. I am in control of my mind and I choose to reject these thoughts." A moment of reflection upon an applicable scripture is all that is needed to renew the mind when accompanied by faith. His purity of mind has another benefit: it keeps his conscience clear.

God Wills That Christians Maintain a Clear Conscience

How much more shall the blood of Christ, who through the eternal Spirit offered himself without spot to God, purge your conscience from dead works to serve the living God? (Heb 9:14)

The human conscience is referred to several times in the epistles. It is not a part of the human mind—which has only two parts, the soul and spirit—but rather is a function of the mind. The mind of the natural man has this function also, but it operates in relativity, comparing the unbeliever's actions and words to his own ideals or some worldly standard such as human law.

In a believer, the Holy Spirit brings to mind those thoughts and actions which contradict God's word (Phil 3:15). "Conviction" is the word that is commonly used to describe this operation, but no such concept is found in the epistles. While the Holy Spirit convicts (declares guilty) the world of its wrongdoing (Jhn 16:8), the members of the body of Christ are no longer counted guilty of sin; in the mind of God, they are holy and without blemish

(Eph 5:27). The illuminating ministry of the Spirit does not condemn the saints; it is a God-given benefit which allows the Christian to maintain a good conscience before God and continue to operate according to His will.

The Christian who evaluates himself, comparing his spiritual things (products) with the spiritual words of scripture (1 Cor 2:13) has the opportunity to make the necessary adjustments if he recognizes ungodliness or sin. This adjustment is known as confession, which simply means to return to agreement with God as described in His written word.

It is worth emphasizing that many of the stumbling stones of the Christian life are not morally impure; neither does rebellion always appear evil. A rightly adjusted conscience assists the spiritual man to discern those things which might not appear obviously sinful, yet cannot be done as to the Lord. There are situations and activities which could lead to temptation, those which are rooted in an impure motive or a negative attitude, and things which are safe for others but not good for one's own spiritual health. In contrast with law, which placed the same external limits on all Jewish people, under grace, each person must determine for himself what kinds of things lead him to develop a poor attitude, corrupt his motives, or tempt him to act independently from God.

A Christian has a good conscience when he recognizes and avoids sin and is quick to return to fellowship with God when he does sin; in other words, he agrees with God rather than denying that sin is sin.

> *If we say that we have no sin, we deceive ourselves, and the truth is not* (operating) *in us. If we confess our sins, he is faithful and just to forgive us* our *sins, and to cleanse us from all unrighteousness. If we say that we have not sinned, we make him a liar, and his word is not* (operating) *in us.*
> (1 Jhn 1:8-10, clarification added)

A Christian with a good conscience before God is sensitive to the tempting thoughts and poor attitudes that precede sin; as he matures, he will return to agreement with God before temptation leads to an episode of carnality. Conversely, a person—whether Christian or not—who continually acts in rebellion to his internal conscience and to external expectations will harden his conscience, making it easier for him to continue in his way (Heb 3:8-15).

> *And Paul, earnestly beholding the council, said, Men* and *brethren, I have lived in all good conscience before God until this day…And herein do I exercise myself, to have always a conscience void of offence toward God, and* toward *men.*
> (Acts 23:1, 24:16)

> *Now the end of the commandment is charity out of a pure heart, and* of *a good conscience, and* of *faith unfeigned…*
> (1 Tim 1:5)

> *This charge I commit unto thee, son Timothy, according to the prophecies which went before on thee, that thou by them mightest war a good warfare; Holding faith, and a good conscience; which some having put away concerning faith have made shipwreck…* (1 Tim 1:18-19)

...holding the mystery of the faith in a pure conscience.
(1 Tim 3:9)

I thank God, whom I serve from my forefathers with pure conscience, that without ceasing I have remembrance of thee in my prayers night and day... (2 Tim 1:3)

Having a good conscience; that, whereas they speak evil of you, as of evildoers, they may be ashamed that falsely accuse your good conversation in Christ. (1 Pet 3:16)

Let love be without dissimulation. Abhor that which is evil; cleave to that which is good... Be not overcome of evil, but overcome evil with good. (Ro 12:9, 21)

The Role of Fear in a Godly Viewpoint

Then had the churches rest throughout all Judaea and Galilee and Samaria, and were edified; and walking in the fear of the Lord, and in the comfort of the Holy Ghost, were multiplied. (Acts 9:31)

As described in the verse above, the church both feared God and was comforted by Him. An accurate and balanced understanding of God Himself is necessary for cultivating a mindset that aligns with His. Living under grace sometimes leads Christians to hold an unbalanced view of God. His gracious forgiveness of sins does not, however, negate His other qualities such as holiness. A holy God hates sin and the attitudes that accompany it. Contrary to the popular claim that fear means nothing more than respect, it actually means *fear*. Christians are to fear the Lord. Jehovah is the Almighty God who is not to be trifled with or taken for granted.

He is not an indulgent grandfather, a romantic boyfriend, or an easy-going buddy. No Christian should characterize him thusly, nor use Him as a curse, caricature, or joke. Living under grace seems to have led some to think that they can be disrespectful or flippant toward God, but grace living is not to be equated with shamelessness. The Old Testament is helpful for correcting irreverence toward God. Its many valuable features include its record of God's words to Israel, its descriptions of His reactions to their conduct, and the many narratives which display His character. His response to those who dishonored Him should remind all men to fear Him. The epistles hold many warnings as well. The saints should never hold the brash mindset that many unbelievers do.

> *There is no fear of God before their eyes.* (Ro 3:18)

> *...because of unbelief they were broken off, and thou standest by faith. Be not highminded, but fear...* (Ro 11:20)

> *Having therefore these promises, dearly beloved, let us cleanse ourselves from all filthiness of the flesh and spirit, perfecting holiness in the fear of God.* (2 Cor 7:1)

> *Submitting yourselves one to another in the fear of God.* (Eph 5:21)

> *Wherefore, my beloved, as ye have always obeyed, not as in my presence only, but now much more in my absence, work out your own salvation with fear and trembling.* (Phil 2:12)

> *Them that sin rebuke before all, that others also may fear.* (1 Tim 5:20)

> *Let us therefore fear, lest, a promise being left us of entering into his rest, any of you should seem to come short of it.* (Heb 4:1)
>
> *Wherefore we receiving a kingdom which cannot be moved, let us have grace, whereby we may serve God acceptably with reverence and godly fear...* (Heb 12:28)
>
> *And if ye call on the Father, who without respect of persons judgeth according to every man's work, pass the time of your sojourning here in fear...* (1 Pet 1:17)
>
> *Honour all men. Love the brotherhood. Fear God. Honour the king.* (1 Pet 2:17)
>
> *While they behold your chaste conversation coupled with fear.* (1 Pet 3:2)

It is important to differentiate godly fear from fleshly fear. The fear of God is not anxiety, which is a pre-occupation with circumstances, possibilities, or matters of discontentment. Christians are not to fear man or the things of this world. Full confidence in the Lord prevents a spiritual man from focusing too heavily on the passing things of this life. Instead, he brings his earthly cares before the Lord rather than ruminating, complaining, or "what-if-ing" about the situation. He does not stumble others with a faithless attitude, doubts, or fleshly reactions. As he adjusts this thinking by setting his mind on applicable truth, his emotions will align with his calm and confident thoughts.

> *There is no fear in love; but perfect love casts out fear, because fear involves torment. But he who fears has not been made perfect in love.* (1 Jhn 4:18 NKJV)

> *For ye have not received the spirit of bondage again to fear; but ye have received the Spirit of adoption, whereby we cry, Abba, Father.* (Ro 8:15)
>
> *For God hath not given us the spirit of fear; but of power, and of love, and of a sound* (saved, i.e. delivered) *mind.* (2 Tim 1:7, clarification added)
>
> *So that we may boldly say, The Lord is my helper, and I will not fear what man shall do unto me.* (Heb 13:6)
>
> *Humble yourselves therefore under the mighty hand of God, that he may exalt you in due time: Casting all your care upon him; for he careth for you.* (1 Pet 5:6-7)

Rather than focusing on the never-ending problems of this life, the spiritual man uses the tools God has given him so that he can abide in God's will regardless of circumstances. Because he holds an appropriate fear of God, he endeavors to limit his mind to things above, such as his provision from God, the truths which apply to his situation, and the work he has to do. Thusly he is able to deal with all things by the power of the Spirit, fulfill the will of God, and hold a mindset of eager watchfulness for the coming of his Savior.

God Wills Watchfulness for Christ's Return

> *But the end of all things is at hand: be ye therefore sober* (saved-minded), *and watch unto prayer.* (1 Pet 4:7, clarification added)

The eager anticipation of the Master's return by his dutiful servants is another outworking of a godly mindset. The Apostles were the last men appointed to human death (1 Cor 4:9). Since then, the rapture has been imminent, meaning that there is no prophetic event that will occur before the rapture of the church; it is ever "at hand."

The watchfulness called for in the epistles is not sign-seeking nor a preoccupation with the machinations of this world; it is not looking for the coming of the Antichrist, nor for the signs which precede Israel's kingdom. Christ's return for the church is without sign or warning; it is vastly different from the almost theatrical return of the judge in wrath, of which there will be manifold signs, the rapture itself being the trigger.

> *Teaching us that, denying ungodliness and worldly lusts, we should live soberly, righteously, and godly, in this present world* (age); *Looking for that blessed hope, and the glorious appearing of the great God and our Saviour Jesus Christ…* (Titus 2:12-13, literal word added)

> *Be patient therefore, brethren, unto the coming of the Lord.* (Ja 5:7a)

> *Even as the testimony of Christ was confirmed in you: So that ye come behind in no gift; waiting for the coming of our Lord Jesus Christ…* (1 Cor 1:6-7)

> *Beloved, now are we the sons of God, and it doth not yet appear what we shall be: but we know that, when he shall appear, we shall be like him; for we shall see him as he is. And every man that hath this hope in him purifieth himself, even as he is pure.* (1 Jhn 3:2-3)

Watchfulness has a special purpose in the Christian life. The eager expectation of the appearance of one's beloved Savior is a reminder to make Him the author of every word, the bishop of every choice, and the shepherd of every experience in life. The Christian who longs for the return of Jesus keeps His appearing foremost in his thoughts. This has a purifying effect on the Christian life: knowing that the last day could be today makes it more precious and perhaps less likely to be wasted.

God Wills That Christians Remember the Brevity of Life

But this I say, brethren, the time is short… (1 Cor 7:29a)

Sharing God's viewpoint includes an acute awareness of the fragility and brevity of human life and the large amount of work to be done. Evil is rampant in every age, and only the power of God can defeat it. The spiritual man must be wise in his use of time and recognize the urgent need to spiritually mature so that he might be useful in God's current program in the short time that he has.

> *Just as a father has compassion on his children, So the LORD has compassion on those who fear Him. For He Himself knows our frame; He is mindful that we are but dust. As for man, his days are like grass; As a flower of the field, so he flourishes. When the wind has passed over it, it is no more, And its place acknowledges it no longer.* (Ps 103:13-16 NASB, see also 1 Pet 1:24)

> *Yet you do not know what your life will be like tomorrow. You are just a vapor that appears for a little while and then vanishes away.* (Ja 4:14 NASB)

> *We then, as workers together with him, beseech you also that ye receive not the grace of God in vain.* (2 Cor 6:1)

Temporal awareness includes redeeming one's time for those things which are eternal. Every thing that a person does takes time; therefore, each person is exchanging time for that activity. The spiritual man understands the importance of redeeming his time and is therefore less likely to waste his time and other resources. Time wisely invested is part of maturity; a mature Christian is stable, prepared, and of great benefit to those around him.

> *...redeeming the time, because the days are evil.* (Eph 5:16)

> *Walk in wisdom toward them that are without, redeeming the time.* (Col 4:5)

A mindset that aligns with the divine viewpoint is vital because the mind is the source of choices and behavior. A Christian who desires to do God's will and appreciates the brevity of life makes himself aware of the many opportunities for ministry around him, acting on them accordingly. He has the same mindset as Jesus had for his own ministry, working at every opportunity to provide spiritual light to others.

> *I must work the works of him that sent me, while it is day: the night cometh, when no man can work. As long as I am in the world, I am the light of the world.* (Jhn 9:4-5)

Adopting God's viewpoint is necessary for spirituality, which in turn is necessary for using time according to God's will. For example, if the church does not make the eternal destiny of the unsaved a priority, the lake of fire is their destination. A Christian who is filled with the Spirit will be filled with the same concern for the lost that God has, and will redeem a portion of his time to speak about the Gospel of Christ, 1 Corinthians 15:1-4.

> *Give none offence, neither to the Jews, nor to the Gentiles, nor to the church of God: Even as I please all* men *in all things, not seeking mine own profit, but the* profit *of many, that they may be saved.* (1 Cor 10:32-33)

> *For though I be free from all* men, *yet have I made myself servant unto all, that I might gain the more. And unto the Jews I became as a Jew, that I might gain the Jews; to them that are under the law, as under the law, that I might gain them that are under the law; To them that are without law, as without law, (being not without law* (lawless) *to God, but under the law to* (in-lawed to) *Christ,) that I might gain them that are without law. To the weak became I as weak, that I might gain the weak: I am made all things to all* men, *that I might by all means save some.* (1 Cor 9:19-22, literal words added)

> *Let your speech* be *alway with grace, seasoned with salt, that ye may know how ye ought to answer every man.* (Col 4:6)

Loving others by making time for them is an outworking of the love that has already been provided by God through the indwelling of regeneration. That love led the Son to willingly give Himself to be put to death on a cross, bearing God's wrath against all the sins of the world in order to redeem those who put Him there (Jhn 10:17-18).

Chapter 3: God Wills that Christians Adopt the Divine Viewpoint

This life is short, and the unpleasant experiences which sometimes accompany Christian service will one day be long forgotten. Think of how quickly the days fly away. One day soon, every person reading this will fly away too. It is God's will that the Christian mindset is in accordance with His; it is, in fact, only reasonable that one should agree with a wise, powerful, loving, and merciful God. One's earthly life, therefore, is to be a joyful, willing sacrifice to Him and for others. A Christian loses nothing by putting God's agenda and the best interests of others ahead of his own. On the contrary, the good works that result from spirituality provide heartening satisfaction here, earn eternal rewards that will multiply the joys of heaven, and bring glory to God.

> *I beseech you therefore, brethren, by the mercies of God, that ye present your bodies a living sacrifice, holy, acceptable unto God,* which is *your reasonable service.* (Ro 12:1)

Each Christian must continually remind himself that God's will for the members of the church is not designed to be a to-do list or a program to "clean up your act." The grace-through-faith program begins with knowing God and His word. This spiritual knowledge and understanding, when believed, manifests those things which God has already provided through spiritual regeneration. The Christian who fills his mind with grace doctrine and denies ungodly thinking will not obey the law of sin (Gal 5:16). As spiritual, he limits his mind for the sake of purity and a clean conscience. He maintains a watchful hope and operates with appropriate fear of offending or shaming his savior. He is motivated by the truth of God's word and therefore redeems his time for things of eternal quality and value. The result of utilizing the mind of Christ is spiritual fruit and works of righteousness which benefit both the body of Christ and the unbelievers in one's sphere of influence. It might seem like a lot to learn and do, but it is all the product of just one thing: spirituality. This supernatural life is to be the normal experience for every person who has been born again by faith in the Gospel of Christ. When the believer reads all about God's will and says, "Yes," to it, God does all the rest.

CHAPTER 4

GOD WILLS THAT CHRISTIANS COMMUNICATE TO HIM

I pray for them: I pray not for the world, but for them which thou hast given me; for they are thine. (Jhn 17:9)

A person who has placed his faith in the Gospel of Christ for salvation (1 Cor 15:1-4) has begun a relationship with God. In every relationship communication is important, and God has provided for His family to communicate to Him by inviting them to pray. God has also provided for the growth of the relationship by giving His written word, the Bible, which accurately records history and the future, describes the way of salvation, and directs the lives of the saints. The Bible declares itself to be sufficient for all things pertaining to life and godliness, and to thoroughly equip the man of God for all good works (2 Tim 3:17, 2 Pet 1:3). It warns that it is not to be added to, whether in writing or by claim, a declaration which stands in opposition to the increasingly popular teaching of continuing revelation (Rev 22:18). God did communicate personally to a tiny number of people in times past, but for Christians, God HAS spoken. To believe otherwise is to disbelieve the Bible, as its claims of sufficiency cannot be reconciled with any perceived need for additional instruction. The Holy Spirit enlightens the mind of the spiritual man to understand biblical doctrine and gives him the wisdom to apply it. His ministry, however, is not always described in a biblically accurate way.

Precision in describing the things of God seems to be less common today than it was in the past. Because words have a meaning and speech is audible, we, the authors, encourage Christians to use care when describing Almighty God. It has become quite common to hear Christians claim to have heard from God or to know His will apart from what is revealed in scripture. Regarding such statements, the authors acknowledge that not every person who says, "God told me…" intends to convey that they heard a voice, received a prophetic directive, or were granted divine inspiration. Oftentimes when a person is asked about his "God told me" statement, he will deny it is divine inspiration. But what else could this personal revelation be? Either God said something or He did not. Either the Bible is sufficient as it claims or it is not. Occasionally one might encounter those who intend to deceive, exaggerate, or misrepresent an experience. What is more likely, however, is that a thought came into a person's mind and that thought was attributed to God.

No biblical word for prayer means two-way communication. Those who mistakenly urge Christians to "listen for God" have left many disappointed or confused at best. The unfulfilled expectation of personalized instruction from God can destroy a person's faith and lead to further deception. It undermines the authority of scripture and attacks the confidence and trust that every Christian should have in it. This is so because it leads to the belief that there is little to gain in studying a 2000-year-old book if one can instead hear a unique message from God today.

The trend toward expecting unique revelation seems to be partially due to a lack of understanding of the teaching role of the Holy Spirit. Imagine, for example, that a Christian is spending a quiet hour reading the Bible. It comes to his mind to start a Bible study. This person might tell others, "God told me to start a Bible study." But God's word already says to study it, to be a teacher to younger believers, and to fellowship with others. This is not new, personalized instruction. It is the Holy Spirit teaching the person how to apply the scriptures he already knows. In another example, a friend who needs to hear the Gospel might come to the mind of a Christian who knows this person is unsaved and that he is to be a witness of the Gospel. The Holy Spirit teaches the spiritual man to apply what he reads in scripture.

Christians can avoid misleading others by learning the specifics of the ministry of the Spirit and describing it with greater care. This world's deceiver, Satan, is very powerful; he can plant things in the mind and—as the god of this age—he can bring them to pass. Nothing, however, is more powerful than the scripture when it is understood and rightly divided. Luring a Christian into trusting anything other than the written word of God is Satan's greatest victory over him. Without the anchor of God's word, he can be drawn away into any number of deceptions, and every Christian sees the effects of this in the culture today.

No man knows God's thoughts apart from His written word. It is known, however, that He does not contradict Himself, nor does the Spirit encourage believers to seek extra-biblical information. God's word can be trusted absolutely, and it informs its readers that God has "changed the program" a few times in history. These changes include the way in which He transmits information. In the past

He used prophets; today the world is blessed with a written record. Recognizing these changes is necessary to understanding God's word (Ro 3:21, Ro 7:6, Ro 16:25-26, Eph 2:13, Col 1:26, Heb 1:1-2, Heb 8:6).

Requests (Asking)

The word "prayer" is used in English as the catch-all word for communicating to God. Prayer can be spoken or silent. It is a one-way act that is to be directed to the Father, in accordance with one's position in the Son, by the power of the Spirit. In other words, a Christian must be spiritual rather than carnal when communicating to his Father in heaven. There are other words that inform the Christian of the various forms of communication; these include supplication, intercession, requests, worship, praise, and the giving of thanks.

One type of communication is the request, usually translated, "ask." This prayer is important to be aware of because several Bible verses promise to give whatever one *asks*, and yet many prayers seem to go unanswered. The solution to this quandary is in the meaning of the word, "ask." Asking is a particular kind of prayer: to "ask" is to make a request for which the answer is known to be "yes." God's word contains the revelation of His will, so when a believer asks in accordance with it, the request is always granted in due time.

> *If any of you lack wisdom, let him **ask** of God, that giveth to all men liberally, and upbraideth not; and **it shall be given him**.* (Jas 1:5)

In the previous verse, James discloses that God always grants requests for wisdom. Wisdom is the proper application of knowledge; it is something that God wills for all Christians. The epistles to the church inform its members about how God's current program operates so that requests can be made and granted. Examples of these requests include asking for a better understanding of scripture, for more opportunities to share the Gospel, and for teaching opportunities. One must know the will of God in order to "ask." Additionally, asking must have a particular character; both the spiritual condition of the petitioner and the nature of the request matter:

> *And this is the confidence that we have in him, that, if we ask any thing **according to his will**, **he heareth us:** And if we know that he hear us, whatsoever we ask, we know that we have the petitions* ("asks") *that we desired* (asked) *of him.* (1 Jhn 5:14-15, literal words added)

> ***If ye abide in me*** (fellowship via spirituality), *and my words abide in you, ye shall ask what ye will, and it shall be done unto you.* (Jhn 15:7, clarification added)

> *And whatsoever ye shall ask in my name, that will I do, that the Father may be glorified in the Son. If ye shall ask any thing **in my name**, I will do it.* (Jhn 14:13-14, see also Jhn 15:16, 16:23-24)

> *But let him ask **in faith**, nothing wavering. For he that wavereth is like a wave of the sea driven with the wind and tossed. For let not that man think that he shall receive any thing of the Lord.* (Jas 1:6-7)

The previous verses teach that requests must be done in accordance with God's will, while abiding in fellowship, and in Christ's name, by faith. To have a good name is to have a commendable character. To ask in someone's name is to ask in accordance with that person's good reputation and with the right motive. A Christian who is operating by faith is abiding in fellowship with God; he is spiritual and not carnal. This means that he is in the spiritual condition which allows his request to be heard. He is aligned with God in agreement, so his request is in accordance with God's will. Not all prayers are heard, but when a spiritual man "asks," that prayer is always granted. The opposite is also true:

> *Ye lust, and have not: ye kill, and desire to have, and cannot obtain: ye fight and war, yet ye have not, because ye ask not. Ye ask, and receive not, because ye ask amiss, that ye may consume it upon your lusts.* (Jas 4:2-3)

> *Now we know that God heareth not sinners: but if any man be a worshipper of God, and doeth his will, him he heareth.* (Jhn 9:31)

> *For the eyes of the Lord are over the righteous, and his ears are open unto their prayers: but the face of the Lord is against them that do evil.* (1 Pet 3:12)

The Christians being addressed in James 4:2 are not failing to obtain because they have not prayed for what they want. Their problem is that they are carnal and not spiritual. They are not asking in accordance with God's will or character but with selfish motives. Similarly, in James 1:6-7 the Christian who prays without believing will not have his request granted either. His doubts reveal that he is using his carnal (fleshly) mind and not the mind of Christ (2 Cor 1:12, 1 Cor 2:16). A spiritual man asks and receives a "yes" to a request because he already knows it is according to God's will and he believes God. He is asking in accordance with the character and good name of Jesus Christ. He is not praying with a selfish or unloving motive, but is communicating to the Father for the sake of advancing His will.

> *And whatsoever we ask, we receive of him, because we keep his commandments, and do those things that are pleasing in his sight.* (1 Jhn 3:22; The word "commandments" refers to the commands to love one another; see John 13:34, 15:9)

It might seem strange that a Christian must ask for something which God already wishes to give him. But God does not force Himself upon anyone either before or after salvation. God is love, and loving acts must be freely given and received. The fact is that not every Christian wants what God wants. Some do not want to study His word, share the Gospel, or serve and help the brethren. Therefore, God waits for the saints to align with His will and request those things which are granted by asking.

Even if a Christian does not know God's will in regard to a need or desire, he may communicate to the Father about it. The Father wants His children to talk to Him, and He will answer or not answer in accordance with His perfect goodness, always acting in their best interest and at the right time. Although it is popular to claim that God answers every prayer with a yes, no, or maybe, there is no scriptural basis for this notion. God is not obligated to answer prayers. Neither can a Christian consider a feeling, impression, or a "sense" of something to be an answer. If a spiritual man makes a request of God and He grants it, it will be obvious.

His Worthy Shape

Worship is another form of communication to God. The word "worship" comes from the Old English "weorthscipe" which approximates through many centuries and languages to "worthy shape;" in other words, God's quality and form is worthy of all glory and honor. Both worship and its close companion, "praise," are forms of communication which facilitate and perpetuate spirituality. The carnal man who rehearses the goodness, mercy and love of God shifts his mind from ruminating upon temptation and trouble; doing so facilitates his return to spirituality. The spiritual man perpetuates his spiritual condition as he reflects upon who God is and what He has done, keeping his mindset on things above rather than being stumbled by his circumstances. When difficulties arise, thoughts of God's character and works stabilize the believer, building confidence and preventing the distress that leads to carnality. Filled with joy and gratitude, the spiritual man acknowledges God's provision for him, leading to more praise and worship.

> *But the hour cometh, and now is, when the true worshippers shall worship the Father in spirit and in truth: for the Father seeketh such to worship him. God is* a *Spirit: and they that worship him must worship* him *in spirit and in truth.*
> (Jhn 4:23-24)

> *For we are the circumcision, which worship God in the spirit, and rejoice in Christ Jesus, and have no confidence in the flesh.* (Phil 3:3)

Considering the importance of worship, it is noteworthy that the word is rarely seen in the letters to the church. A mere three verses inform the Christian of the character and nature of worship: It is a function of the spirit (as opposed to the soul or body) and its contents must be true. One cannot say he is worshipping God if what is being said about God is not accurate. The ability to know God is a function of the human spirit (1 Cor 2:11). Therefore, New Testament worship is spiritual and must be founded in knowledge and understanding of Him. For example, it is not worship if the topic is not God but is instead self, as in "I." Worship occurs when a spiritual man frames his mind upon the *character* of God and communicates those truths back to God. Similarly, to praise God is to frame the mind upon His *works* and speaks well of them. When one person praises another, he speaks only of the one he is praising. He does not talk about himself and call it praise.

Worship and praise may be spoken, sung, or thought. Their purpose is to rehearse truth, encourage, give thanks, and joyfully proclaim to God how good He is and how wonderful are His works. It is worth noting that the songs mentioned in the following verses are called spiritual; this confirms that they come from knowing God, not merely from the emotions of the soul (although emotional reactions are often stirred by reflection upon truth.) In Ephesians 5, spiritual song and thankfulness are contrasted with a fleshly way of coping which does not provide deliverance from the cares of the world:

> *And be not drunk with wine, wherein is excess* (no deliverance); *but be filled with the Spirit; Speaking to yourselves in psalms and hymns and spiritual songs, singing and making melody in your heart to the Lord; Giving thanks always for all things unto God and the Father in the name of our Lord Jesus Christ...* (Eph 5:18-20, literal words added)

> *Let the word of Christ dwell in you richly in all wisdom; teaching and admonishing one another in psalms and hymns and spiritual songs, singing with grace in your hearts to the Lord.* (Col 3:16)

Christian praise and worship are not the same as the external expressions of Old Testament worship because the source of Christian worship is the regenerated human spirit. Singing or playing music can occur during worship but these activities themselves do not constitute worship. The spiritual condition of the worshipper and the accuracy of the content are the only criteria of worship, not the mode. Singing religious music is not necessarily worship because many hymns and songs contain false doctrine; worship must be in truth. Neither are one's words and songs counted by God to be worship if the one speaking them is carnal; the product of one's flesh brings no glory to God (Ro 14:23). A Christian who recognizes that he is carnal or is not certain of his spiritual condition would do well to remain quiet during corporate worship time and allow the expressions of others to minister to him. The truths expressed in the worship music can facilitate his return to spirituality.

Conversely, a Christian can enter worship as a spiritual man, but the music or lyrics stir the body and soul to the point of shifting him from a spiritual expression to a fleshly one. Consider the possibility that if a particular type of music leads a person to feel about and react to church music the same way that he does to secular music, this indicates a shift from the realm of the spirit to the flesh. Judging one's spiritual condition is necessary in order to actually worship God rather than to just act worshipful. Discernment must be exercised in music just as it must be in reading books, listening to teaching, and any other way in which God's word is communicated.

Thanksgiving

In every thing give thanks: for this is the will of God in Christ Jesus concerning you. (1 Thes 5:18)

The word thanksgiving is a wonderful word. It is a compound of two words; "good" and "grace." It literally means to tell God how good His grace is! The giving of thanks is an acknowledgment that all one has is from God and is unearned; the Christian who offers thanksgiving to God recognizes the undeserved favor which he has received and is calling it good. Thankfulness is vitally important for the believer to remain in the will of God, for it provides deliverance from carnal (fleshly) mindedness which is characterized by attitudes of self-pity, discouragement, and discontentment, for example. The Christian need not wait until he "feels" thankful; he can begin thanking God, and by confessing the truth of the many good things God provides, these truths minister encouragement back to him. Even in unhappy circumstances, there are things for which one can be thankful. As a Christian considers his many blessings, dissatisfaction with his current circumstances lessens in comparison to God's present and future provision.

> *For all things are for your sakes, that the abundant grace might through the thanksgiving of many redound to the glory of God.* (2 Cor 4:15)
>
> *...and there must be no filthiness and silly talk, or coarse jesting, which are not fitting, but rather giving of thanks.* (Eph 5:4 NASB)
>
> *Giving thanks always for all things unto God and the Father in the name of our Lord Jesus Christ...* (Eph 5:20)
>
> *Be careful for nothing; but in every thing by prayer and supplication with thanksgiving let your requests* (asks) *be made known unto God.* (Phil 4:6)
>
> *Rooted and built up in him, and stablished in the faith, as ye have been taught, abounding therein with thanksgiving.* (Col 2:7)
>
> *And let the peace of God rule in your hearts, to the which also ye are called in one body; and be ye thankful.* (Col 3:15)
>
> *And whatsoever ye do in word or deed, do all in the name of the Lord Jesus, giving thanks to God and the Father by him.* (Col 3:17)
>
> *Continue in prayer, and watch in the same with thanksgiving...* (Col 4:2)

Unanswered Prayer

Unanswered prayer might seem like a strange problem to have in a relationship between a beloved child and an all-powerful God.

It can be a source of frustration, anxiety, confusion, and sorrow. It might seem as if a carrot is being dangled that can never be reached. A Christian might think to himself, "God can do anything, so why won't He do this?" Many prayers are not answered because the person asking is an unbeliever with no standing before God (Jhn 9:31, 1 Pet 3:12), but in regard to Christians, there are a few things which can hinder prayer.

A supplication (a prayer for a need or a want to be met) or an intercessory prayer (on behalf of others) might be unanswered because the request is not according to God's will. Requests (ask) are for those things which are known to be God's will, but Christians are not promised an answer to other types of prayer. Those things which are not addressed in scripture, such as personal choices in liberty, can certainly be prayed for, but they might not be granted. This is important to remember because an unanswered prayer does not necessarily mean that God is displeased or that fellowship has been broken. Knowing God's promises and understanding His objectives in the current program of grace will help the believer to avoid discouragement. A believer should never pray for a sign or a feeling when seeking an answer to prayer. If God answers a prayer, it will be obvious. If no answer or solution comes, get the best advice possible and make a decision in wisdom, the granting of which *is* promised in scripture.

Some prayers are not answered for the protection of the saint. A human being cannot see the future and does not know the outcome of what he wishes to have or to happen. God is omniscient and knows what the result of the prayer will be. Because He loves His children, He might deny a supplication because it is not wise, beneficial, glorifying, or best in the long-term. A prayer that seems to have gone unanswered might also be a matter of timing and will be answered later. It is always wise to align with God's will and timing. The believer can say, "God if this is not according to your will or if it is not the right time, please ignore this prayer!" (Ja 4:15).

Motive also hinders prayer. God knows that human beings are often merely seeking relief. Although in His mercy He might provide relief from a difficult situation, God does not exist to relieve Christians of their circumstances. Instead, He has provided the faith system so that the saints might bear them and develop maturity. A human lifetime on earth is short, and there is much to do. The things done here will affect eternity, and God desires the best eternity possible for His children. Therefore, He does not always fix things; it is more important for a saint to grow in faith, to learn to weather adversity with patience, and perhaps to recognize his own role in the problem so that it does not happen again.

An overlooked issue in regard to communicating to God is that sometimes prayer goes unanswered because one already has access to that for which one is praying. Although it might appear as if a prayer has not been heard, the answer might already be in God's word. For example, a feeling of peace is one quality of the fruit of the Spirit. It is available at all times, by faith. Asking for peacefulness will not bring it; the agitated or anxious Christian must know from the scriptures that it is already available—and believe it. Only by faith can a Christian experience that which he has already been promised. Failing to know God's word and promises to the church is to choose to live in spiritual poverty rather than withdrawing the riches from God's treasury. Prayer is meant to be like a telephone line that is always open. A believer can communicate to God throughout the day, intermittently assessing his spiritual condition so that his communication will be in faith and in accordance with God's will as taught in His written word.

> *Rejoicing in hope; patient in tribulation; continuing instant in prayer...* (Ro 12:12)
>
> *Praying always with all prayer and supplication in the Spirit, and watching thereunto with all perseverance and supplication for all saints...* (Eph 6:18)
>
> *Continue in prayer, and watch in the same with thanksgiving...* (Col 4:2)
>
> *Pray without ceasing.* (1 Thes 5:17)
>
> *I exhort therefore, that, first of all, supplications, prayers, intercessions,* and *giving of thanks, be made for all men...* (1 Tim 2:1)
>
> *But ye, beloved, building up yourselves on your most holy faith, praying in the Holy Ghost...* (Jude 1:20)

Christians can petition the Father for help, intercede on behalf of others, pour out their hearts to Him without fear, and talk to Him about anything. God already knows every feeling and thought; the fact that the saints can approach Him personally and be heard is a special gift to the church (Heb 4:14-16). God wills that His children avail themselves of this privilege and benefit from the spiritual intimacy that prayer provides.

CHAPTER 5

GOD WILLS THAT CHRISTIANS BE FILLED WITH HIS FULLNESS

> *For of His fullness we have all received, and grace upon grace.*
> (Jhn 1:16 NASB)

God desires that all men be saved through faith in the Gospel. He wills for believers to study His word in order to know Him, to communicate to Him, and to think like Him, viewing the world as it really is. Christians are to operate by faith in the promises of God, enabling the realization of those promises by the indwelling Holy Spirit. The Christian who knows, believes, and yields to the teachings of grace-through-faith is a spiritual man, filled with the fulness of God. In this condition he is able to produce works which are of an acceptable quality. Attempting to use other means to live the Christian life is to render oneself powerless, for the power of God is imparted through faith in His word.

> *Wherefore also we pray always for you, that our God would count you worthy of* this *calling, and fulfil all the good pleasure of* his *goodness, and the work of faith with power...*
> (2 Thes 1:11)

The Spiritual Man is Filled

> *And these things write we unto you, that your joy may be full.* (1 Jhn 1:4)

The Bible describes more than one kind of spiritual filling. In Acts 2, for example, the Apostles were filled in order to speak in languages they had not been taught. This type of filling was a kind of mental control. The control that God exercised before the completion of the canon of scripture was necessary for the Apostles and New Testament prophets to teach those things which laid the foundation of the church (1 Cor 3:10, Eph 2:19-20). The foundation was soundly laid, established, and preserved in writing for use in Christian living; therefore, the present-time filling of the believer does not necessitate mental control, but is instead a filling up of what is lacking. Examples of such lacking could be in boldness, motivation, contentment, or patience. The spiritual man believes God's promises to provide these things and yields himself. Because the word of God is living and active, the believer is filled. The filling of the Spirit is a condition that exists when a Christian operates by faith; it perfects the spiritual man, enabling him to do God's will.

> *For this cause we also, since the day we heard* it, *do not cease to pray for you, and to desire that ye might be filled with the knowledge of his will in all wisdom and spiritual understanding...* (Col 1:9)

> *These things have I spoken unto you, that my joy might remain in you, and* that *your joy might be full.* (Jhn 15:11)

Chapter 5: God Wills that Christians be Filled with His Fullness

> *And to know the love of Christ, which passeth knowledge, that ye might be filled with all the fulness of God.* (Eph 3:19)

> *And now come I to thee; and these things I speak in the world, that they might have my joy fulfilled in themselves… And I have declared unto them thy name, and will declare it: that the love wherewith thou hast loved me may be in them, and I in them.* (Jhn 17:13, 26)

It is beyond comprehension that the Christian is "filled with all the fullness of God," but it is something that the Son asked of the Father and was granted. Christ took upon Himself humanity so that through His sacrifice those who believe will share in the joyous quality of life that exists in eternity (Jhn 17:5). This eternal quality of life is available to the Christian whenever he is spiritual. The Christian who reads, for example, that he can turn his cares over to God and enjoy a peace that surpasses understanding, appropriates that benefit by faith (Phil 4:6-7). It is God's will that His children enjoy and display the benefits that Jesus Christ won on the cross.

> *Whereby are given unto us exceeding great and precious promises: that by these* (promises) *ye might be partakers of the* (quality of the) *divine nature, having escaped the corruption that is in the world through lust.* (2 Pet 1:4, clarification added)

> *But ye* are *a chosen generation, a royal priesthood, an holy nation, a peculiar people; that ye should shew forth the praises* (virtues) *of him who hath called you out of darkness into his marvellous light…* (1 Pet 2:9, synonym added)

> *Always bearing about in the body the dying of the Lord Jesus, that the life also of Jesus might be made manifest in our body. For we which live are alway delivered unto death for Jesus' sake, that the life also of Jesus might be made manifest in our mortal flesh.* (2 Cor 4:10-11)
>
> *For in him dwelleth all the fulness of the Godhead bodily. And ye are complete in him...* (Col 2:9-10a)
>
> *And hath put all things under his feet, and gave him to be the head over all things to the church, Which is his body, the fulness of him that filleth all in all.* (Eph 1:22-23)
>
> *Till we all come in the unity of the faith, and of the knowledge of the Son of God, unto a perfect man, unto the measure of the stature of the fulness of Christ...* (Eph 4:13)

Astonishingly, the saints are not only filled with His fullness, they are Christ's fullness as well! He is the head of a new creation, the spiritual entity known as the body of Christ. Each Christian has a new position as a member of that body (Eph 2:14-16). As a Christian operates according to God's will, he is fulfilling his purpose as God is filling any lacking in him. Living consistently in the fulness of God literally fills the believer's life. He will cease to view his life and his "religion" separately; his Christian life is his life.

Spiritual Fruit

> *But the fruit of the Spirit is love, joy, peace, longsuffering, gentleness, goodness, faith, Meekness, temperance...* (Gal 5:22-23a)

Spiritual fruit is spiritual. It consists of the love of God and the many aspects of that love. Producing spiritual fruit is the alternative to producing works of the flesh. The works of the flesh are manifest and obvious, but the outward appearance of spirituality can be faked: a person can appear to be peaceful and patient while feeling very differently inside. Therefore, spiritual fruit-bearing is not a proof of salvation; it is a measure to oneself of one's spiritual condition. The Christian who evaluates (judges) himself and recognizes sin can immediately return to fellowship with God through confession, which is to agree with Him in regard to that sin.

Spiritual fruit-bearing is an operation of the mind. The mind is comprised of the human spirit, which knows things, and the soul, which is the seat of volition (will) and emotion. When grace teaching is learned and appropriated by faith, the spiritual man will experience peace instead of anxiety. Instead of hatred and bitterness he feels love and forgiveness; instead of irritation he feels patience; instead of self-pity he feels thankful. He is emanating the character of God and is able to reject the influence of his flesh, which is full of cravings and self-concern, the devil, who is full of lies, and the world, which is full of cares and distractions; he is free (Gal 5:1). The following are a small sampling of verses describing God's bountiful spiritual fruit:

> *With all lowliness and meekness, with longsuffering, forbearing one another in love…* (Eph 4:2)
>
> *Let your moderation be known unto all men.* (Phil 4:5a)

Not that I speak in respect of want: for I have learned, in whatsoever state I am, therewith to be content. I know both how to be abased, and I know how to abound: every where and in all things I am instructed both to be full and to be hungry, both to abound and to suffer need. I can do all (spiritual) *things through Christ which strengtheneth me.* (Phil 4:11-13, clarification added)

But as touching brotherly love ye need not that I write unto you: for ye yourselves are taught of God to love one another. (1 Thes 4:9)

Now we exhort you, brethren, warn them that are unruly, comfort the feebleminded, support the weak, be patient toward all men. *See that none render evil for evil unto any* man; *but ever follow that which is good, both among yourselves, and to all* men. *Rejoice evermore.* (1 Thes 5:14-16)

And having food and raiment let us be therewith content… But thou, O man of God, flee these things; and follow after righteousness, godliness, faith, love, patience, meekness. (1 Tim 6:8, 11)

That the aged men be sober, grave, temperate, sound in faith, in charity, in patience. (Titus 2:2)

To speak evil of no man, to be no brawlers, but *gentle, shewing all meekness unto all men.* (Titus 3:2)

> *And beside this, giving all diligence, add to your faith virtue; and to virtue knowledge; And to knowledge temperance; and to temperance patience; and to patience godliness; And to godliness brotherly kindness; and to brotherly kindness charity. For if these things be in you, and abound, they make you that ye shall neither be barren nor unfruitful in the knowledge of our Lord Jesus Christ.* (2 Pet 1:5-8)

The spiritual man uses scriptures such as these to evaluate his mindset and motives in order to make the necessary adjustments to his thinking. It is God's will that Christians live as spiritual men, and spirituality cannot be accomplished by the willpower of the flesh. The Christian who believes that God will produce these virtues within him will enjoy the fullness of God's spiritual blessing, be a blessing to others, and bring glory to God.

The Spiritual Man is Led

A Christian might sometimes be heard saying, "I feel led to…," or "I think that I am being led…" Being led by the Spirit of God is not a feeling or something one imagines to be happening. It is not an experience, a sign, nor a sensing of something. All such ideas are inventions built around two short verses containing the word "led" which teach nothing even close to these ideas.

Being led is a fact that exists when a Christian is operating in accordance with his position in Christ. This book does not detail the mechanics of "in Christ" truth, but suffice it to say that to operate in one's position in Christ, one must be spiritual. A spiritual man is spiritual because he is directing his faith toward the doctrines which instruct him in the operation of the Christian life. When he allows himself to be informed by grace teaching and applies them to his life, those truths are leading him via the Holy Spirit. If an issue is not addressed in scripture, the spiritual man asks God for wisdom. He might also consult with wise counsel and make a decision in liberty. In doing so, he is operating by spiritual power as a mature son of God.

> *For as many as are led by the Spirit of God, they are* (operating in their position as) *the sons of God.* (Ro 8:14, clarification added)

Consider, for example, a Christian who is considering further education. He might ask himself, "Can I afford it? How will this affect my family? Will it significantly impact my career?" Unbelievers make similar decisions all the time; Christians have no crystal ball for their decisions and God does not promise one, but He does promise wisdom. Spiritual leading is not toward or away from attending school; God leads the believer to use His grace-through-faith program in *every* circumstance. Christians must trust God's provision of wisdom through His word to be sufficient for their needs. To believe what God says and operate accordingly is to be led by it.

In a time of trial, the Spirit might bring to remembrance a Bible verse that calls the Christian to be thankful in all things. He believes that he can be thankful even in a trial and shifts his mind to consider those things for which he is thankful. His gratitude reminds him that God has brought him through trials many times before, and that reminder gives him patience to endure. Therefore, instead of being occupied with the difficulties of the trial, becoming downcast or complaining, he bears the trial as a spiritual man and is not drawn into carnality. Instead of responding to the principle (law) of sin, he is led by what he knows in his spirit (Ro 7:23). He recognizes that the trial draws him closer to God and that his spirit-filled condition is a testimony to those around him; this fills him with even more joy and thanksgiving! His spiritual condition leads to more fruit-bearing because he believes God and is led to respond in accordance with what he believes.

> *...and if by the Spirit ye are led, ye are not under law.*
> (Gal 5:18 YLT; the law of sin, according to 5:16-17)

To Quench or Grieve the Spirit Nullifies God's Fullness

> *Quench not the Spirit. Despise not prophesyings* (divine declarations). *Prove all things; hold fast that which is good.*
> (1 Thes 5:19-21, clarification added)

A spiritual man has said, "Yes," to God; in other words, he is cooperating with God's will as revealed in scripture. As spiritual, he enjoys the fullness of his benefits in Christ because he is neither quenching nor grieving the Spirit of God. To quench the Spirit means to say, "No," to God. The Holy Spirit wishes to produce something, but rather than yield to God's will, the Christian ignores what he knows to be true or resists what he knows he is to do.

Quenching the work of the Spirit leaves only one alternative: operating in the flesh. The man who refuses to cooperate will rapidly become carnal, operating according to the law of sin within him. He must renew his mind with the truth, comparing his mindset to the spiritual teachings of scripture and adjusting himself in order to return to agreement with God. The Holy Spirit then resumes the production of God's character in the believer, teaching and reminding him of what is right, and empowering him to do it. He is again filled with the fulness of God.

> *Which things also we speak, not in the words which man's wisdom teacheth, but which the Holy Ghost teacheth; comparing spiritual things* (products) *with spiritual* (words). (1 Cor 2:13, clarification added)

A Christian can evaluate his spiritual condition by asking himself if there is something that he has not done. He might recognize, for example, that he is intimidated or fearful of losing something and therefore he has been silent regarding the Gospel of Christ. He can ask himself things such as, "Am I withholding truth from an unsaved acquaintance or fellowship from a Christian friend? Am I aware of the physical and spiritual needs of the believers in my church and in my life? Am I busy with activities that have no eternal value? Is my Christian service focused on trying to solve the symptoms of sin rather than sin's true solution? Is my giving directed in accordance with God's clear instruction regarding His work for the church?" These questions are not to pressure the flesh into a "try harder; do more" mindset, but are for self-evaluation. If quenching is recognized, it can be replaced with yieldedness to God.

Grieving the Spirit

> *And grieve not the holy Spirit of God, whereby ye are sealed unto the day of redemption.* (Eph 4:30)

The Christian who is quenching the Spirit might not yet be actively committing sin. If he continues to be fleshly-minded, however, he will sin, and it grieves God to be exposed to sin. The remedy for grieving the Spirit is the same as it is for quenching; the carnal Christian must change his mind in regard to the sin, returning to agreement with God (confession). It is the truth that sets the Christian free from the power of sin, the lure of the world, and the deception of the enemy (Jhn 8:32, 36). Sin can be deceptive because it is not necessarily something that is obviously evil by human standards. To sin is to act independently of God, therefore, whatever is not of faith is sin; in other words, whenever a Christian is not operating by the faith system, he is operating according to the principle (law) of sin. His works are of the same quality as sin (Ro 14:23).

An interesting implication of the warning against grieving the Spirit is that it reveals the Christian's security in Christ. The Spirit would not need to be grieved if He could leave, but His sealing ministry is a promise. God has sealed each saint with His Spirit unto the day of ultimate redemption from these sin-infested bodies. God keeps His promises and, therefore, no person who has been born again can be "un-saved," "un-indwelt," or no longer God's child for any reason or by any means. A believer can, however, fail to cooperate with God and operate by the sin principle, living as a carnal man (Eph 1:13, 2 Cor 1:22).

Sin is Never God's Will

My little children, these things write I unto you, that ye sin not. (1 Jhn 2:1a)

Salvation is freedom from the penalty, power, and ultimately the presence of sin. Some seem to misunderstand this, concluding that since the Christian is sealed and secure, he is free to sin. Some even believe that grace teaching encourages sin. On the contrary, God's grace enables the Christian *not* to sin. The carnal Christian needs more grace teaching, not less, in order to understand the spiritual power to which he has access. Jesus did not die for sins for the purpose of having dishonor heaped upon His sacrifice. The Bible is clear: God wills that His children do not sin:

> *What shall we say then? Shall we continue in sin, that grace may abound? God forbid. How shall we, that are dead to sin, live any longer therein? ...Knowing this, that our old man is crucified with him, that the body of sin might be destroyed, that henceforth we should not serve sin. ...Let not sin therefore reign in your mortal body, that ye should obey it in the lusts thereof.* (Ro 6:1-2, 6, 12)

> *Awake to righteousness, and sin not; for some have not the knowledge of God: I speak* this *to your shame.*
> (1 Cor 15:34)

> *And they that are Christ's have crucified the flesh with the affections and lusts.* (Gal 5:24)

> *Be ye angry, and sin not...* (Eph 4:26a)

No student of the Bible can rightly claim that grace teaches licentiousness. On the contrary, a Christian who is quenching or grieving the Spirit cannot at the same time be doing the will of God. The normal expectation of the Christian is that he take full advantage of the power of the grace-through-faith program by knowing God, His word, and His way.

The Christian who desires to live by faith must continue to remind himself that spirituality is not a to-do list or a "try harder; do more" program. It is a deliberate mental effort to take the divine viewpoint as one's own, and to trust and believe God for daily operation. The spiritual Christian is empowered by God's grace; he is operating by the faith system of Christ and not by the power of his flesh. These are the only two operating systems; a Christian is always using either one or the other (Ro 6:16; 8:6-8). The Christian who is abiding in the truth of God's word by faith cannot at the same time sin (Gal 5:16, 1 Jo 3:6, 9). God's grace is in vain if the Christian does not utilize it to live in the deliverance that was purchased on the cross. The Christian who, throughout his day, briefly returns his mind to grace doctrine can fulfill God's will by emanating His character in whatever task he must do.

> *We then,* as *workers together* with him, *beseech* you *also that ye receive not the grace of God in vain.* (2 Cor 6:1)

> *Thou therefore, my son, be strong in the grace that is in Christ Jesus.* (2 Tim 2:1)

Paul As a Pattern

> *That he would grant you, according to the riches of his glory, to be strengthened with might by his Spirit in the inner man…* (Eph 3:16)

Sinful works of the flesh are not the only things which rob God of the glory He deserves; it is perhaps equally common that Christians do good things the wrong way. Nobody will be fooled by manifest wickedness, but many are fooled by law, for example. Law is an external system that works like a fence; it depends upon a person's willpower to stay on the correct side of the fence. The Old Testament believers were supposed to utilize the Law of Moses; they were not indwelt by the Holy Spirit and did not have the power of God in the inward man. They were to try their best to obey the limits of the Law. Due to the nature of man, however, rules actually entice man to sin. Therefore, the law system, which used commandments to highlight man's sinfulness, displayed man's weakness exactly as God intended. This, in turn, pointed to the need for a savior from sin.

> *Therefore by the deeds of the law there shall no flesh be justified in his sight: for by the law is the knowledge of sin.* (Ro 3:20)
>
> *Was then that which is good* (the law) *made death unto me? God forbid. But sin, that it might appear sin, working death in me by that which is good; that sin by the commandment might become exceeding sinful.* (Ro 7:13)
>
> *For what the law could not do, in that it was weak through the flesh, God sending his own Son in the likeness of sinful flesh, and for sin, condemned sin in the flesh...* (Ro 8:3)

After His resurrection, Jesus Christ unveiled the workings of the new grace-through-faith program to Paul. Paul traveled to Jerusalem and taught it to the other Apostles who then had the task of weaning the Jewish believers from the Mosaic Law and other Judaic religious practices. The Jewish Christians had to be convinced to abandon lifelong practices and live instead by the power of the Spirit. To follow Christ now meant to follow what the resurrected Christ had taught to Paul (1 Cor 11:1) Paul's letters to the church call believers to utilize the new way of life, filled with the fullness of God.

But I certify you, brethren, that the gospel which was preached of me is not after man. For I neither received it of man, neither was I taught it, *but by the revelation of Jesus Christ. And I went up by revelation, and communicated unto them that gospel which I preach among the Gentiles … And when James, Cephas, and John, who seemed to be pillars, perceived the grace that was given unto me, they gave to me and Barnabas the right hands of fellowship; that we* should go *unto the heathen, and they unto the circumcision.* (Gal 1:11-12; 2:2a; 2:9)

*Wherefore I beseech you, be ye followers of **me**.* (1 Cor 4:16)

Be ye followers of me, even as I also am *of Christ* (resurrected). *Now I praise you, brethren, that ye remember me in all things, and keep the ordinances, **as I** delivered them to you.* (1 Cor 11:1-2, clarification added)

*Howbeit for this cause I obtained mercy, that **in me first** Jesus Christ might shew forth all longsuffering, **for a pattern** to them which should hereafter believe on him to life everlasting.* (1 Tim 1:16)

*Brethren, be followers together of **me**, and mark them which walk so as ye have **us** for an ensample.* (Phil 3:17)

Furthermore then we beseech you, brethren, and exhort you *by the Lord Jesus, that as ye have received **of us** how ye ought to walk and to please God, so ye would abound more and more.* (1 Thes 4:1)

> *And ye became followers of us, and of the Lord, having received the word in much affliction, with joy of the Holy Ghost...* (1 Thes 1:6)
>
> *Not because we have not power, but to make ourselves an ensample unto you to follow us.* (2 Thes 3:9)

The other Apostles learned and wrote about the new teachings also, passing them on to Christians everywhere.

> *...even as our beloved brother Paul also according to the wisdom given unto him hath written unto you; As also in all his epistles, speaking in them of these things...* (2 Pet 3:15b-16a)

Unbelievers can do good things. They can help, give, sacrifice, and much more. Spirituality is different because God is producing within the believer things which are of an acceptable *quality*. Operating as a spiritual man is what fulfills God's will so that one's efforts are not just empty religious works and temporary earthly improvements. Through spirituality, God works in and through the Christian, filling him with His fullness and leading him to share the good news of salvation, to provide for the needs of the saints, and to glorify Him.

CHAPTER 6

GOD WILLS THAT CHRISTIANS BE HOLY AS HE IS HOLY

Wherefore gird up the loins of your mind, be sober, and hope to the end for the grace that is to be brought unto you at the revelation of Jesus Christ; As obedient children, not fashioning yourselves according to the former lusts in your ignorance: But as he which hath called you is holy, so be ye holy in all manner of conversation; Because it is written, Be ye holy; for I am holy. (1 Pet 1:13-16)

The words saint, holy, and sanctify are variations of the same Greek word. A saint is one who has been made a member of the spiritual entity called the body of Christ through spiritual baptism; his faith in the Gospel, 1 Corinthians 15:1-4, qualified him for this exalted position. Holiness (sanctification) refers to the fact that he is set apart to God; his set-apart condition is also known as his position in Christ. By exercising faith in the truth, a Christian can operate in accordance with his holy position:

Sanctify them through thy truth: thy word is truth. (Jhn 17:17)

And for their sakes I sanctify myself, that they also might be sanctified through the truth. (Jhn 17:19)

Holiness (sanctification) means to be separated and set apart to something. A full explanation of this doctrine is beyond the scope of this book, but a few things are helpful to begin to understand holiness. In the mind of God, the believer has "changed locations;" he has been moved from his position "in Adam," and transferred to the body of Christ with Jesus Christ as the head (1 Cor 15:22, Col 1:13, 18, Eph 4:15, 5:23). This spiritual entity was newly created to include every born-again person, uniquely setting the church apart to God for His purposes in grace.

Sanctification is sometimes described as being set apart from sin. It is true that a spiritual man who is living in accordance with his position in Christ cannot at the same time be sinning, but biblical sanctification is better understood as being set apart *to* something than *from* something. Consider the fact that God is holy. He never changes and He was holy before sin existed, therefore, defining holiness is not best explained with reference to sin.

God always acts in accordance with His nature: everything He does identifies exactly with who He is. With that in mind, when a Christian is holy as God is holy, he is not merely avoiding sin; he is operating in accordance with his exalted position in Christ. His manner of life matches his status, and separation from sin is a result. Sanctification/holiness is to live out who one is in Christ, working out by faith what God has worked within. Holiness uses one's possessions in Christ (such as his deliverance from sin) to accomplish the intended outcome of living as a spiritual man.

As an example, imagine a Christian who spends much time watching television at home; he is not engaged in sinful activity; he is spiritual, thankful, and full of love in his heart for the Lord, at least for a time. If there is no outworking of God's will in his life, no evangelism, no help for the saints, no effort toward deeper Bible knowledge, that person is not operating as a member of the body. The church is described as a body because body parts work together. The Christian who does not live as a functional body part will not maintain spirituality. His time at home on the sofa will become slothful carnality at best, and could even disqualify him for useful service if he persists (1 Cor 9:24-27). He has not lost his salvation, but there will be tears in heaven when he realizes the rewards that were lost because he did not believe that God's will was better than what his soul desired. (Rev 21:4).

The Word Cleanses and Sanctifies Within

Now ye are clean through the word which I have spoken unto you. (Jhn 15:3)

A Christian is cleansed from sin and holy (sanctified) at the very moment of his salvation. God views the members of the body of Christ to be pure, clean, and blameless. They are to operate in accordance with His view, without spot or blemish from the world, and without wrinkle from sitting and doing nothing.

That he might sanctify and cleanse it with the washing of water by the word, That he might present it to himself a glorious church, not having spot, or wrinkle, or any such thing; but that it should be holy and without blemish. (Eph 5:26-27, see also Jhn 17:17-19. The word "washing" is actually a noun and is better translated laver or wash-basin. The word is the wash-basin of water; it is the cleansing agent. This is not a reference to baptism.)

> *Do all things without murmurings and disputings: That ye may be blameless and harmless, the sons of God, without rebuke, in the midst of a crooked and perverse nation, among whom ye shine as lights in the world; Holding forth the word of life...* (Phil 2:14-16a)
>
> *In the body of his flesh through death, to present you holy and unblameable and unreproveable in his sight...* (Col 1:22)
>
> *To the end he may stablish your hearts unblameable in holiness before God, even our Father, at the coming of our Lord Jesus Christ with all his saints.* (1 Thes 3:13)
>
> *...be diligent that ye may be found of him in peace, without spot, and blameless...* (2 Pet 3:14b)

The cleansing of the human spirit at the moment of spiritual birth (regeneration) is once for all in regard to salvation. Sins have been paid and their penalty was borne by Christ. However, the sin principle remains operative in the human body, warring against the soul, the seat of volition. Grace doctrine renews the Christian mind, framing it on things above so that the spiritual man might avoid temptation and banish ungodly thoughts. Although holiness is not defined by avoiding sin, holiness does exclude sin; therefore, the scripture warns Christians to avoid sin in order to maintain holiness:

> *Having therefore these promises, dearly beloved, let us cleanse ourselves from all filthiness of the flesh and spirit, perfecting holiness in the fear of God.* (2 Cor 7:1)

For this is the will of God, your sanctification: that you should abstain from sexual immorality; that each of you should know how to possess his own vessel in sanctification and honor, not in passion of lust, like the Gentiles who do not know God; that no one should take advantage of and defraud his brother in this matter, because the Lord is *the avenger of all such, as we also forewarned you and testified. For God did not call us to uncleanness, but in holiness. Therefore he who rejects* this *does not reject man, but God, who has also given us His Holy Spirit.* (1 Thes 4:3-8 NKJV)

And that ye put on the new man, which after God is created in righteousness and true holiness. Wherefore putting away lying, speak every man truth with his neighbour: for we are members one of another. Be ye angry, and sin not: let not the sun go down upon your wrath… Let him that stole steal no more: but rather let him labour, working with his *hands the thing which is good, that he may have to give to him that needeth. Let no corrupt communication proceed out of your mouth, but that which is good to the use of edifying, that it may minister grace unto the hearers. And grieve not the holy Spirit of God, whereby ye are sealed unto the day of redemption. Let all bitterness, and wrath, and anger, and clamour, and evil speaking, be put away from you, with all malice…* (Eph 4:24-26, 28-31)

Wherefore laying aside all malice, and all guile, and hypocrisies, and envies, and all evil speakings… (1 Pet 2:1)

God's Will

> *Not rendering evil for evil, or railing for railing: but contrariwise blessing; knowing that ye are thereunto called, that ye should inherit a blessing. For he that will love life, and see good days, let him refrain his tongue from evil, and his lips that they speak no guile: Let him eschew* (shun) *evil, and do good; let him seek peace, and ensue* (follow) *it.* (1 Pet 3:9-11, synonyms added)

The warnings not to gossip, steal, speak evil, and so on, could be used as laws; a Christian could use personal will-power as many unbelievers do in an attempt to conform to social morality. Exercising will-power can produce a certain amount of change, but its source is the sin principle, the only alternative to spirituality. Spirit-filling effects changes in the inward man, producing things of a different quality. Just as it requires faith and biblical study to change years or decades of sin, so too must a Christian stop "trying to be good," and instead learn to look to grace doctrine in dependence and faith. A Christian can begin by regularly asking himself, "What is my attitude about this? What is my motive?" Allowing the Spirit to critique the inward man initiates the process of learning to differentiate spirituality from living on "auto-pilot," meaning to simply go through life without discerning the source and quality of one's actions. Actions resulting from spirituality bring glory to God because they are produced by Him. Therefore, the spiritual man can be called holy as God is holy.

Faith and Reckoning: Quality and Power

> *At that day ye shall know that I am in my Father, and ye in me, and I in you.* (Jhn 14:20)

Every Christian is called to be both spiritual and holy. These two ideas can be described as "Christ in me" and "me in Christ." Upon believing the Gospel, the believer's human spirit is cleansed from sin (regenerated), making it habitable for God (1 Cor 6:17). When he operates by faith in God's promises, he emanates the character of God and is, in a small way, a partaker in the divine nature. The products of his Spirit-filled condition are of an acceptable quality. This is "Christ in me."

> *Whereby are given unto us exceeding great and precious **promises: that by these** ye might be partakers of the divine nature, having escaped the corruption that is in the world through lust.* (2 Pet 1:4, emphasis added)

Faith in a promise makes it actual in the believer's experience. For example, in a difficult situation, a saint is to believe the promise of God for patience and deal with the circumstance as a spiritual man instead of becoming agitated or losing his temper.

Reckoning is a similar doctrine, but is slightly different than exercising faith. Whereas spirituality is a product of regeneration, reckoning is related to one's position in the body of Christ (also known as spiritual baptism). To reckon is to count something true, so belief is still a factor. However, things that are reckoned are established facts and possessions; Christians already have these things because of their position in Christ. They are not made actual in experience but have already been accomplished. A Christian is able to use these things when he reckons (counts) them to be true. For example, when one reckons himself to be dead with Christ, he does not experience death. He is simply identified with Christ; this is "me in Christ." Reckoning accesses resurrection power, enabling the Christian to operate as if he is dead to sin and no longer under its power, because this has been accomplished by Christ. It is the alternative to operating according to the law of sin. The Christian who reckons himself dead to sin is able to operate free from the dominion of sin, using the power that raised Christ Jesus from the dead. Because a Christian can say, "I have Christ in me," he can be spiritual, emanating God's character. The Christian who understands "I am in Christ" and reckons it true, operates in accordance with the holy position provided by his spiritual baptism (Ro 6:3-13). He uses his possessions, such as his deliverance from sin, to do God's will, living out what has been accomplished for him and within him.

> *But if the Spirit of him that raised up Jesus from the dead dwell in you, he that raised up Christ from the dead shall also quicken your mortal bodies by his Spirit that dwelleth in you.* (Ro 8:11)

> *And declared* to be *the Son of God with power, according to the spirit of holiness, by the resurrection from the dead...* (Ro 1:4)

> *That I may know him, and the power of his resurrection, and the fellowship of his sufferings, being made conformable unto his death...* (Phil 3:10)

> *Buried with him in* (spiritual) *baptism, wherein also ye are risen with* him *through the faith* (system) *of the operation of God, who hath raised him from the dead.* (Col 2:12, clarification added)

The value of making the distinction between faith and reckoning may not be immediately apparent, but it will become so as a Christian recognizes these doctrines in scripture and uses them. To be spiritual by faith is to emanate God's character, thereby experiencing the fruit of the Spirit: it is to be at peace, and to be patient, kind, and forgiving toward others. It is to be full of love, thankfulness, and joy regardless of circumstances. To be holy in practice is to use a set of spiritual tools in order to have a successful Christian life. Using these tools is often described as the "walk" of the believer.

Walk Worthy: Practical Holiness

> *If we live in the Spirit, let us also walk in the Spirit.* (Gal 5:25)

Upon salvation, a new believer is transferred from his position "in Adam" and set apart to God into a new position "in Christ" (Col 1:13, 1 Cor 15:45). After initial salvation, the spiritual man is called to be holy (sanctified) in daily living and the call to do so is: "Walk worthy." Worthiness is a word picture of a balanced scale, the two sides of which weigh the same amount; in other words, the Christian's conduct and choices match or "weigh the same" as his position. His life reflects God's view of him in Christ.

> *That ye might walk worthy of the Lord unto all pleasing, being fruitful in every good work, and increasing in the knowledge of God…* (Col 1:10)

> *That ye would walk worthy of God, who hath called you unto his kingdom and glory.* (1 Thes 2:12)
>
> *I therefore, the prisoner of the Lord, beseech you that ye walk worthy of the vocation wherewith ye are called…* (Eph 4:1)

A series of verses in Ephesians and several other verses call Christians to walk worthy of their position and describe some of the results of holiness.

> *This I say therefore, and testify in the Lord, that ye henceforth walk not as other Gentiles walk, in the vanity of their mind…* (Eph 4:17)
>
> *And walk in love, as Christ also hath loved us, and hath given himself for us an offering and a sacrifice to God for a sweetsmelling savour.* (Eph 5:2)
>
> *For ye were sometimes darkness, but now* are ye *light in the Lord: walk as children of light…* (Eph 5:8)
>
> *See then that ye walk circumspectly, not as fools, but as wise…* (Eph 5:15)
>
> *That the righteousness of the law might be fulfilled in us, who walk not after the flesh, but after the Spirit…So then they that are in the flesh cannot please God.* (Ro 8:4, 8)
>
> *That ye may walk honestly toward them that are without, and* that *ye may have lack of nothing.* (1 Thes 4:12)

> *Wherefore also we pray always for you, that our God would count you worthy of* this *calling, and fulfil all the good pleasure of* his *goodness, and the work of faith with power...* (2 Thes 1:11)

> *But if we walk in the light, as he is in the light, we have fellowship one with another, and the blood of Jesus Christ his Son cleanseth us from all sin. ... If we confess our sins, he is faithful and just to forgive us* our *sins, and to cleanse us from all unrighteousness.* (1 Jhn 1:7, 9)

> *But whoso keepeth his word, in him verily is the love of God perfected: hereby know we that we are* (operating) *in him. He that saith he abideth in him ought himself also so to walk, even as he walked.* (1 Jhn 2:5-6, clarification added)

> *I rejoiced greatly that I found of thy children walking in truth, as we have received a commandment from the Father... And this is love, that we walk after his commandments. This is the commandment, That, as ye have heard from the beginning, ye should walk in it.* (2 Jhn 1:4, 6)

Walking worthy results from reckoning; things that are reckoned have already been accomplished and the spiritual man has already been enabled to do them. Therefore, the believer does not pray for what he already has; he simply counts to be true what God says is so. If a Christian prays for somethings that is already accomplished, it is a prayer that God cannot answer because He has already done this perfectly and cannot do more. This is why knowledge of the scripture is imperative. To walk worthy, one must know what he already has in Christ and live as if it is so, because in the mind of God it is so. God desires that His children walk in holiness so that He might count them worthy in practice as they already are in position. Every Christian is called to partner with God in bringing the Gospel of Christ to the lost, and to love Him by loving His children—his brothers and sisters in Christ. Every Christian has been liberated from the power of sin; he can now choose to be empowered by God's grace and obey God's will.

What Does Holiness Look Like?

Many things about holy living are ordinary and not necessarily great "religious" works. Simple things like minding one's own business, holding one's tongue, and working to support oneself facilitate holiness. A Christian is less likely to be tempted to sin when he is busy taking care of his own life and taking the ministry opportunities that he is likely to be presented with nearly every day. Christians are to do all things as to the Lord, taking literally Jesus' statement, "...*without me ye can do nothing.*" (Jhn 15:5b)

> *And that ye study to be quiet, and to do your own business, and to work with your own hands, as we commanded you; That ye may walk honestly toward them that are without, and that ye may have lack of nothing.* (1 Thes 4:11-12)

> *Now them that are such we command and exhort by our Lord Jesus Christ, that with quietness they work, and eat their own bread.* (2 Thes 3:12)

> *Put them in mind to be subject to principalities and powers, to obey magistrates, to be ready to every good work...* (Titus 3:1)

A conversation that one of the authors had with a friend who wanted to learn how to live the Christian life provides an illustration of doing things as to the Lord. It was suggested to the friend to do his laundry as if he was literally doing it "for the Lord," and report his experience. The friend reported that he approached the laundry the next day with much thought; he made certain he had sorted it properly and that he had all the needed supplies. After drying, he neatly folded each piece and placed items on hangers with care. He agreed that the word "deliberate" best described the exercise. He reported feeling joyful and honored by the idea of doing his Lord's laundry. His attitude toward the laundry that day was a result of his mindset and love for his Savior. His task was completely ordinary; what was new was its source. By faith, joy had filled his heart, and a routine chore became an act of love. Cultivating the mind of Christ while completing daily duties is a way to learn to be Spirit-filled, which in turn produces works that God counts as holy.

Strong Words for the Rebellious

When holiness is lacking, God is not amused. Paul had harsh words for the unproductive. Peter included busybodies (time wasters) in a list of evildoers with murderers (1 Pet 4:15)! Christians who were doing what they should not and not doing what they should are not offered a pat on the back and sympathy. "At least you tried," and "A for effort" are not in the grace vocabulary. A holy God expects Christians to successfully avoid sin, work, and minister because He has provided the means to do so. Paul did not sugar-coat rebellion against God, which is what acting independently from Him amounts to.

For we hear that there are some which walk among you disorderly, working not at all, but are busybodies. (2 Thes 3:11)

And withal they learn to be idle, wandering about from house to house; and not only idle, but tattlers also and busybodies, speaking things which they ought not. (1 Tim 5:13)

But if any provide not for his own, and specially for those of his own house, he hath denied the faith, and is worse than an infidel. (1 Tim 5:8)

For even when we were with you, this we commanded you, that if any would not work, neither should he eat. (2 Thes 3:10)

Let no corrupt communication proceed out of your mouth, but that which is good to the use of edifying, that it may minister grace unto the hearers. (Eph 4:29)

Every Christian is a minister and must live accordingly if he wishes to please his Lord and Savior. God's grace includes the power which enables believers to do His will.

And now, brethren, I commend you to God, and to the word of his grace, which is able to build you up... (Acts 20:32a)

...but I laboured more abundantly than they all: yet not I, but the grace of God which was with me. (1 Cor 15:10b)

Not that we are sufficient of ourselves to think any thing as of ourselves; but our sufficiency is of God... (2 Cor 3:5)

But we have this treasure in earthen vessels, that the excellency of the power may be of God, and not of us. (2 Cor 4:7)

God is able to make all grace abound toward you; that ye, always having all sufficiency in all things, may abound to every good work… (2 Cor 9:8)

And he said unto me, My grace is sufficient for thee: for my strength is made perfect in weakness. Most gladly therefore will I rather glory in my infirmities, that the power of Christ may rest upon me. Therefore I take pleasure in infirmities, in reproaches, in necessities, in persecutions, in distresses for Christ's sake: for when I am weak, then am I strong. (2 Cor 12:9-10)

Whereof I was made a minister, according to the gift of the grace of God given unto me by the effectual working of his power. (Eph 3:7)

Thou therefore, my son, be strong in the grace that is in Christ Jesus. (2 Tim 2:1)

Let us therefore come boldly unto the throne of grace, that we may obtain mercy, and find grace to help in time of need. (Heb 4:16)

Wherefore we receiving a kingdom which cannot be moved, let us have grace, whereby we may serve God acceptably with reverence and godly fear… (Heb 12:28)

Holiness Includes Separateness

And if any man obey not our word by this epistle, note that man, and have no company with him, that he may be ashamed. (2 Thes 3:14)

Obedience to holiness sometimes necessitates separation from people. It should go without saying that a Christian is to be separate from and not yoked with an unbeliever. Christians will encounter unsaved persons in the course of daily business and are to interact for the sake of evangelism. To do so is not yoking; Christians must exercise discernment as to their level of involvement with the unsaved, keeping the furtherance of the Gospel as a priority.

Separation from other Christians is sometimes necessary also. Because the sin principle continues to operate in a Christian just as it does in every person, a Christian can be carnal and commit any sin (1 Cor 5:1, 12-13; 1 Pet 4:15). A Christian who will not reckon himself dead to sin but instead continues in it cannot at the same time be in fellowship with God. Therefore, he is not in fellowship with the body of Christ either. It can be painful to withdraw from a carnal Christian, but a human relationship cannot be placed above God. Separation can be short-term, such as rapidly ending a telephone call so as not to give ear to gossip, or long-term due to ongoing works of the flesh. The refusal of a Christian to repent of false doctrine is a common cause of separation. As in all things, God's will for every person is good. It is no help whatsoever to the carnal Christian to be allowed to feel comfortable in his rebellion against God. Separation, of course, presumes that efforts to correct have been attempted.

*Now I beseech you, brethren, mark them which cause divisions and offences **contrary to the doctrine** which ye have learned; and avoid them.* (Ro 16:17)

I wrote unto you in an epistle not to company with fornicators: …with such an one no not to eat. For what have I to do to judge them also that are without? do not ye judge them that are within? But them that are without God judgeth. Therefore put away from among yourselves that wicked person. (1 Cor 5:9, 11b-13)

Be ye not unequally yoked together with unbelievers: for what fellowship hath righteousness with unrighteousness? and what communion hath light with darkness? And what concord hath Christ with Belial? or what part hath he that believeth with an infidel? And what agreement hath the temple of God with idols? for ye are the temple of the living God; as God hath said, I will dwell in them, and walk in them; and I will be their God, and they shall be my people. Wherefore come out from among them, and be ye separate, saith the Lord, and touch not the unclean thing; and I will receive you… (2 Cor 6:14-17)

And have no fellowship with the unfruitful works of darkness, but rather reprove them. For it is a shame even to speak of those things which are done of them in secret. (Eph 5:11-12)

Abstain from all appearance of evil. And the very God of peace sanctify you wholly; and I pray God your whole spirit and soul and body be preserved blameless unto the coming of our Lord Jesus Christ. (1 Thes 5:22-23)

> *A man that is an heretick after the first and second admonition reject; Knowing that he that is such is subverted, and sinneth, being condemned of himself.* (Titus 3:10-11)
>
> *Perverse disputings of men of corrupt minds, and destitute of the truth, supposing that gain is godliness: from such withdraw thyself.* (1 Tim 6:5)
>
> *Now we command you, brethren, in the name of our Lord Jesus Christ, that ye withdraw yourselves from every brother that walketh disorderly, and not after the tradition which he received of us.* (2 Thes 3:6)
>
> *But shun profane and vain babblings: for they will increase unto more ungodliness.* (2 Tim 2:16)
>
> *Having a form of godliness, but denying the power thereof: from such turn away.* (2 Tim 3:5)

To be holy is to be separated unto God in position and to live accordingly in practice. One day all Christians will be set apart to God permanently. The church is to take seriously its command to live a sanctified life in the mean time. A Christian who damages his testimony by compromising himself might become of no use to God and certainly is not bringing Him glory. John writes strongly that to overlook sin is the equivalent of committing the sin oneself:

> *For he that biddeth him God speed is partaker of his evil deeds.* (2 Jhn 1:11)

The church is to be crystal clear about God's opinion of sin and not excuse itself from taking a stand against it. It is not grace, nor "the love of Jesus" to overlook wicked deeds, acts of rebellion, unbelief, or compromise; doing so could encourage those practicing sin or spreading heresy to justify to themselves their actions. Purity is vital to Christian living. To be pure is to be undefiled, untainted, uncorrupted, and uncompromised. Holiness includes purity of mind and purity in conduct.

> *Prove all things; hold fast that which is good.* (1 Thes 5:21)

> *Let no man despise thy youth; but be thou an example of the believers, in word, in conversation, in charity, in spirit, in faith, in purity.* (1 Tim 4:12)

> *The elder women as mothers; the younger as sisters, with all purity.* (1 Tim 5:2)

> *Flee also youthful lusts: but follow righteousness, faith, charity, peace, with them that call on the Lord out of a pure heart.* (2 Tim 2:22)

> *Who gave himself for us, that he might redeem us from all iniquity, and purify unto himself a peculiar people, zealous of good works.* (Titus 2:14)

> *But the wisdom that is from above is first pure, then peaceable, gentle,* and *easy to be intreated, full of mercy and good fruits, without partiality, and without hypocrisy.* (Ja 3:17)

> *Seeing ye have purified your souls in obeying the truth through the Spirit unto unfeigned love of the brethren, see that ye love one another with a pure heart fervently…* (1 Pet 1:22)

> *This second epistle, beloved, I now write unto you; in both which I stir up your pure minds by way of remembrance:* (2 Pet 3:1)

> *Beloved, now are we the sons of God, and it doth not yet appear what we shall be: but we know that, when he shall appear, we shall be like him; for we shall see him as he is. And every man that hath this hope in him purifieth himself, even as he is pure.* (1 Jhn 3:2-3)

> *Draw nigh to God, and he will draw nigh to you. Cleanse your hands, ye sinners; and purify your hearts, ye double minded.* (Ja 4:8)

> *Little children, keep yourselves from idols. Amen.* (1 Jhn 5:21)

What Holiness is Not

Holiness/sanctification is a position reckoned by God and the outworking of an internal spiritual condition; it means to be separated *to* God, although separating *from* some people and some things of the world is often a result. Holy separation does not mean that Christians hide from the world (Jhn 17:5); One must engage unbelievers to a certain degree in order to witness to them. Similarly, with regard to carnal believers, separation does not mean that no effort is made to help. The wayward Christian can be rebuked in love and offered truth, but the spiritual Christian must be careful not to adopt his mindset, join him in sin or seem to condone it.

> *Brethren, if a man be overtaken in a fault, ye which are spiritual, restore such an one in the spirit of meekness; considering thyself, lest thou also be tempted.* (Gal 6:1)

> *Lay hands suddenly on no man, neither be partaker of other men's sins: keep thyself pure.* (1 Tim 5:22)

Christian separation does *not* mean avoiding someone due to feeling hurt, offended, irritated or "turned off" by another Christian. Breaking fellowship or refusing to forgive after a disagreement or perceived slight is never in accordance with God's will. Christian unforgiveness is so rampant that it has a name: "Christian 'ghosting,'" a reference to discontinuing fellowship and disappearing. Holiness is never a refusal to forgive, something which no Christian can defend. Neither should separation be considered permanent; the door to restoration should always be open, awaiting the repentance of the carnal believer. When fellowship with the errant saint resumes, forgiveness by those affected is not a private mental exercise, but a full restoration of the relationship among the members of the body. Failing to do so compounds the problem, providing an opening for Satan to take further advantage of those who are not utilizing the mind of Christ. Forgiveness will be covered further in Chapter 8.

> *...so instead* of further rebuke, now *you should rather* graciously *forgive and comfort and encourage him, to keep him from being overwhelmed by excessive sorrow. Therefore I urge you to reinstate him in your affections and reaffirm your love for him. For this was my purpose in writing, to see if you would stand the test, whether you are obedient and committed to following my instruction in all things. If you forgive anyone anything, I too forgive* that one; *and what I have forgiven, if I have forgiven anything, has been for your sake in the presence of* and with the approval of *Christ, to keep Satan from taking advantage of us; for we are not ignorant of his schemes.* (2 Cor 2:7-11 AMP)

Holiness Is Not Just About Self

It might not occur to a Christian that he is exposing a holy God to everything that he says or does. What grief it must cause our heavenly Father to have to endure our sins, having sent the Son to die to provide us with deliverance from them. How it grieves the Holy Spirit, who enables the bearing of spiritual fruit, when a Christian decides instead to produce the works of the flesh. What a tragedy to trample underfoot the magnificent work of Christ so that one might return to wallow in the mire of sin.

> *Now therefore ye are no more strangers and foreigners, but fellowcitizens with the saints, and of the household of God; And are built upon the foundation of the apostles and prophets, Jesus Christ himself being the chief corner* stone; *In whom all the building fitly framed together groweth unto an holy temple in the Lord: In whom ye also are builded together for an habitation of God through the Spirit.* (Eph 2:19-22)

> *Know ye not that your bodies are the members of Christ? shall I then take the members of Christ, and make* them *the members of an harlot? God forbid. ... Flee fornication. Every sin that a man doeth is without the body; but he that committeth fornication sinneth against his own body. What? know ye not that your body is the temple of the Holy Ghost* which is *in you, which ye have of God, and ye are not your own? For ye are bought with a price: therefore glorify God in your body, and in your spirit, which are God's.*
> (1 Cor 6:15, 18-20)

> *Know ye not that ye are the temple of God, and* that *the Spirit of God dwelleth in you? If any man defile the temple of God, him shall God destroy; for the temple of God is holy, which* temple *ye are.* (1 Cor 3:16-17)

A Christian has been set apart (holy, sanctified) in the spiritual organism called the body of Christ immediately upon regeneration through faith in the Gospel of Christ. He can practice holiness (sanctification) as soon as he is taught to do so. Failing to walk worthy of his position can spread his poor attitude or ungodly behavior to others. The writer of Hebrews reminds his readers that they have the ability to be spiritual and holy; therefore, they should use it in order to avoid spreading ungodly attitudes to others.

> *Follow peace with all* men, *and holiness, without which no man shall see the Lord: Looking diligently lest any man fail of the grace of God; lest any root of bitterness springing up trouble* you, *and thereby many be defiled…* (Heb 12:14-15)

Every Christian is a representative of Jesus Christ. The Christian who does not live in accordance with his position in Christ is tarnishing the reputation of Christ himself. One's personal attitude and conduct can defame the church and hinder the work of its members. Ungodly choices can cause other believers to stumble into sin themselves. Unbelievers and even some carnal Christians will take the opportunity to use a Christian's words and poor behavior to speak against God.

> *Giving no offence in any thing, that the ministry be not blamed…* (2 Cor 6:3)

> To be *discreet, chaste, keepers at home, good, obedient to their own husbands, that the word of God be not blasphemed.* (Titus 2:5)

> *Only let your conversation* (conduct as a citizen of heaven) *be as it becometh the gospel of Christ...* (Phil 1:27a, definition added)

The Christian life is a deliberate life. The spiritual man has taken the time to evaluate his condition and has adjusted himself to the Holy Spirit. He then has choices to make regarding his actions. As he considers his options, he takes God's view as his own view. He counts to be true the things that God says are true, regardless of how things appear. He counts himself dead to sin and lives in accordance with his exalted position in Christ, just as God lives in accordance with who He is. Through His sufficient written word, God enables willing Christians to do all that He asks, thereby fulfilling His will.

> *According as his divine power hath given unto us all things that* pertain *unto life and godliness, through the knowledge of him that hath called us to glory and virtue...* (2 Pet 1:3)

> *Therefore, my beloved brethren, be ye stedfast, unmoveable, always abounding in the work of the Lord, forasmuch as ye know that your labour is not in vain in the Lord.* (1 Cor 15:58)

CHAPTER 7

GOD WILLS THAT CHRISTIANS LIVE EXTRAORDINARY LIVES

Whereof I am made a minister, according to the dispensation of God which is given to me for you, to fulfil the word of God; Even *the mystery which hath been hid from ages and from generations, but now is made manifest to his saints: To whom God would make known what* is *the riches of the glory of this mystery among the Gentiles; which is Christ in you, the hope of glory: Whom we preach, warning every man, and teaching every man in all wisdom; that we may present every man perfect in Christ Jesus…* (Col 1:25-28)

God wills that all men be saved; He offers the free gift of salvation from sin to all, and grants it to all who believe the Gospel of Christ, 1 Corinthians 15:1-4. Beyond initial salvation, God calls the saints to know Him through His word, to share His viewpoint, to communicate to Him, and to enjoy fellowship with Him. He wills that Christians are filled with His fullness, rapidly incorporating spiritual truth into practice, freely enjoying all He has provided in grace, and living as mature, wise, stable adults as a testimony to His greatness. To do so is to live an extraordinary life.

Maturity

> ... *always labouring fervently for you in prayers, that ye may stand perfect and complete in all the will of God.*
> (Col 4:12b)

To spiritually mature is to operate as a spiritual man with increasing consistency and in more areas of life. A mature Christian is not thrown off-course by the trials of life, but maintains his walk of faith, trusting the Lord to provide and guide regardless of circumstances. No other believers in history have been able to spiritually mature because nobody has been spiritually alive since the fall of Adam and Eve into sin; it is unique to the church. Because pre-resurrection believers operated by personal willpower, they could only do their best. The Israelites, for example, were to continually meditate on the law in order to improve their performance (Psalm 1:2). The grace program of the church is much better.

> *For the law made nothing perfect, but the bringing in of a better hope* did; *by the which we draw nigh unto God.*
> (Heb 7:19)

> *God having provided some better thing for us, that they without us should not be made perfect.* (Heb 11:40)

Bible verses referring to maturity often describe the spiritual man as perfected or perfect, although it does not mean sinless perfection. Jesus prayed to the Father for the maturity of those who would believe. The mature Christian displays the love which characterizes that of the divine persons.

Chapter 7: God Wills that Christians Live Extraordinary Lives

I in them, and thou in me, that they may be made perfect in one; and that the world may know that thou hast sent me, and hast loved them, as thou hast loved me. (Jhn 17:23)

Maturing spiritually is a choice and is in no way automatic or guaranteed. It follows no particular progression and is a direct result of a Christian's efforts to study, believe, and use grace doctrine. A Christian can choose to ignore the Bible, learn nothing, and never witness, teach, or help another believer; every Christian has observed this and knows it is so. The letters to the church are filled with correction to wayward saints and pleas to forsake carnality for truth. Whether due to ignorance, disinterest, rebellion, or deception, immaturity is a common condition among those who are born again.

> *Not that I have already obtained* it *or have already become perfect* (completely mature), *but I press on so that I may lay hold of that for which also I was laid hold of by Christ Jesus. Brethren, I do not regard myself as having laid hold of* it *yet; but one thing* I do: *forgetting what* lies *behind and reaching forward to what* lies *ahead, I press on toward the goal for the prize of the upward call of God in Christ Jesus. Let us therefore, as many as are perfect* (relatively mature), *have this attitude; and if in anything you have a different attitude, God will reveal that also to you; however, let us keep living by that same* standard *to which we have attained* (in our position). (Phil 3:12-16 NASB, clarification added)

The spiritual man studies the Bible with faith, looking to the Holy Spirit to illuminate his mind so that he can understand and apply God's word to his life. His maturity increases as he uses what he knows in new experiences and circumstances, making him more usable to the Lord. However rare it might be in practice, maturity is the biblical expectation for every Christian, whose destiny is to be conformed to the image of God the Son. Every occurrence in life provides an opportunity for the transforming power of grace through faith to increase the Christlikeness of the yielded believer.

> *For whom he did foreknow, he also did predestinate to be conformed to the image of his Son, that he might be the firstborn* (preeminent) *among many brethren.* (Ro 8:29, clarification added)

> *Being confident of this very thing, that he which hath begun a good work in you will perform it until the day of Jesus Christ...* (Phil 1:6)

> *For the perfecting of the saints, for the work of the ministry, for the edifying of the body of Christ: Till we all come in the unity of the faith, and of the knowledge of the Son of God, unto a perfect man, unto the measure of the stature of the fulness of Christ...But speaking the truth in love, may grow up into him in all things, which is the head, even Christ...* (Eph 4:12-13, 15)

Grace teaches the Christian to discern his spiritual condition. The spiritual man's willingness to learn and change course when necessary facilitates his spiritual maturity.

> *For the grace of God that bringeth salvation hath appeared to all men, Teaching us that, denying ungodliness and worldly lusts, we should live soberly, righteously, and godly, in this present world* (age); (Titus 2:11-12, literal word added)

> *All scripture is given by inspiration of God, and is profitable for doctrine, for reproof, for correction, for instruction in righteousness: That the man of God may be perfect, throughly furnished unto all good works.* (2 Tim 3:16-17)

> *But whoso keepeth his word, in him verily is the love of God perfected: hereby know we that we are* (operating) *in him.* (1 Jhn 2:5, clarification added; this is about maturity, not proof of salvation. One's salvation rests in whether or not one believes the Gospel of Christ, 1 Cor 15:1-4.)

On judgment day, the Christian who has cooperated with God as a spiritual man will not be ashamed or afraid to face his Lord; he can approach the judgment seat with boldness because his yieldedness allowed God to work in and through him.

> *No man hath seen God at any time. If we love one another, God dwelleth in us, and his love is perfected in us. ... Herein is our love made perfect, that we may have boldness in the day of judgment: because as he is, so are we in this world.* (1 Jhn 4:12, 17)

The writers of the epistles had strong words for the spiritually immature:

> *And I, brethren, could not speak unto you as unto spiritual, but as unto carnal, even as unto babes in Christ. I have fed you with milk, and not with meat: for hitherto ye were not able to bear it, neither yet now are ye able. For ye are yet carnal: for whereas there is among you envying, and strife, and divisions, are ye not carnal, and walk as* (natural) *men?* (1 Cor 3:1-3, clarification added)

> *For when for the time ye ought to be teachers, ye have need that one teach you again which* be *the first principles of the oracles of God; and are become such as have need of milk, and not of strong meat. For every one that useth milk is unskilful in the word of righteousness: for he is a babe. But strong meat belongeth to them that are of full age,* even *those who by reason of use have their senses exercised to discern both good and evil.* (Heb 5:12-14)

> *Brethren, do not be children in your thinking; yet in evil be infants, but in your thinking be mature.* (1 Cor 14:20 NASB)

> *That we* henceforth *be no more children, tossed to and fro, and carried about with every wind of doctrine, by the sleight of men,* and *cunning craftiness, whereby they lie in wait to deceive...* (Eph 4:14)

Just like today, some in the early church needed to change their hearts and redirect their love toward the Father and His will, rather than toward the attractions of the world and the flesh.

> *Love not the world, neither the things* that are *in the world. If any man love the world, the love of the Father is not* (operating) *in him. For all that* is *in the world, the lust of the flesh, and the lust of the eyes, and the pride of life, is not of the Father, but is of the world. And the world passeth away, and the lust thereof: but he that doeth the will of God abideth for ever* (into the age). (1 Jhn 2:15-17, clarification and literal words added)

> *Dearly beloved, I beseech* you *as strangers and pilgrims, abstain from fleshly lusts, which war against the soul...* (1 Pet 2:11)

Spiritual maturity provides improvement to every aspect of the believer's life. Coping better with tragedy, loving others more, and quickly repenting of sin are examples of its benefits. But maturity is not simply for the benefit of the believer; like all aspects of spirituality, it also brings glory to the Lord.

> *Make you perfect in every good work to do his will, working in you that which is wellpleasing in his sight, through Jesus Christ; to whom* be *glory for ever and ever. Amen.* (Heb 13:21)

The mature Christian's faith grows as he sees how God is using his yieldedness. Trying times are among the best for perfecting one's faith and maturity. As God brings the Christian through the trials of life, it becomes impossible to imagine going through such things without Him.

> *You see that faith was working with his works, and as a result of the works, faith was perfected...* (Ja 2:22 NASB)

> *But the God of all grace, who hath called us unto his eternal glory by Christ Jesus, after that ye have suffered a while, make you perfect, stablish, strengthen, settle* you. (1 Pet 5:10)

Enjoying the satisfaction that results from partnership with God, weathering difficulties with grace, and becoming conformed to the image of Christ is an extraordinary way to live.

"Stablished"

...That ye be not soon shaken in mind, or be troubled...
(2 Thes 2:2a)

Christians understand that salvation provides deliverance from the penalty of sin, which is everlasting separation from God as a resident of the lake of fire. What some might not know is that deliverance has also been granted from temptation and the power of sin in daily living. This principle is found in a wonderful word from the King James translation of the Bible. The word "stablish" might appear to be an alternate spelling of the word "establish," but it does not mean to place, set-up, or initiate, but to make firm and stabilize.

The sin principle that operates in every person is a contributor to the emotional reactions and instability which rob Christians of the peace, joy, and self-control that Christ won on the cross. Stablishing is an effect that grace teaching has on the human soul, the seat of emotion and volition (will). Exiting the emotional rollercoaster that sometimes rules the soul is a remarkable result of spiritual maturity.

The soul differs greatly from the human spirit which is aligned with and indwelt by God. Recognizing this distinction is necessary for Christian living. When the human soul is influenced primarily by events and experiences, the swing from one emotional reaction to another can make life difficult. In reacting to sunshine or rain, a happy song or a sad one, candy or kale, the soul is lifted or depressed, sometimes many times in a day. Therefore, the soul needs to be "stablished" by looking first to God and then viewing circumstances from His perspective.

Chapter 7: God Wills that Christians Live Extraordinary Lives

> *For all the promises of God in him* are *yea, and in him Amen, unto the glory of God by us. Now he which stablisheth us with you in Christ, and hath anointed us,* is *God…* (2 Cor 1:20-21)

Being led by emotions, opinions, and ungodly influences instead of by the truth is to be "soulish," translated "natural" or "sensual" in the King James version of the Bible. God's truth stabilizes the soul when a Christian chooses to believe it rather than to primarily focus on circumstances, feelings, desires, or other people. When a spiritual man studies a passage of scripture about Christian living, the Holy Spirit illuminates his human spirit to its meaning and teaches its application. The spiritual man trusts God's character and believes the promises that he sees in the passage. For example, in a tragic or stressful situation he could allow his emotions to overwhelm him, surrendering his confidence and strength. He could become carnal, responding to the desires of his flesh, making rash decisions and operating like he did when he was unsaved. If he chooses instead to use what he knows from scripture, he is stabilized and able to go through the trial in a God-honoring way. He is not bound by the principle of sin and its effect on his soul.

A believer is to display the extraordinary nature of the Christian life by living out the many benefits of spiritual maturity. The Christian who uses the truths of grace doctrine will free himself from soulish responses, enjoying instead a life that is grounded and settled. The stablishing of the soul is one of the real and practical ways in which the truth makes Christians free (Jhn 8:32, 36). The people who interact with a stabilized Christian will appreciate and enjoy him, and his testimony will be strong and credible.

> *Now to him that is of power to stablish you according to my gospel...* (Ro 16:25a)

> *To the end he may stablish your hearts* (the seat of decision-making) *unblameable in holiness before God, even our Father, at the coming of our Lord Jesus Christ with all his saints.* (1 Thes 3:13, clarification added)

> *Comfort your hearts, and stablish you in every good word and work.* (2 Thes 2:17)

> *But the Lord is faithful, who shall stablish you, and keep you from evil.* (2 Thes 3:3)

> *Be ye also patient; stablish your hearts: for the coming of the Lord draweth nigh.* (Ja 5:8)

The word translated "established" in the following three verses is the word "stablish."

> *For I long to see you, that I may impart unto you some spiritual gift, to the end ye may be established...* (Ro 1:11)

> *And sent Timotheus, our brother, and minister of God, and our fellowlabourer in the gospel of Christ, to establish you, and to comfort you concerning your faith...* (1 Thes 3:2)

> *Wherefore I will not be negligent to put you always in remembrance of these things, though ye know* them, *and be established in the present truth.* (2 Pet 1:12)

The word "stablish" in the following verse is not the same word as in the previous verses, but the verse is teaching the stabilizing effect of maturity.

> *Rooted and built up in him, and stablished in the faith, as ye have been taught, abounding therein with thanksgiving.* (Col 2:7)

Other scriptures related to stability call Christians to be grounded, unmoveable, and steadfast. Being a mature, stable Christian has many secondary benefits such as strength, good decision-making, doctrinal fidelity, confidence, good works, and comfort to the soul.

> *Therefore, my beloved brethren, be ye stedfast, unmoveable, always abounding in the work of the Lord, forasmuch as ye know that your labour is not in vain in the Lord.* (1 Cor 15:58)

> *Be on the alert, stand firm in the faith, act like men, be strong.* (1 Cor 16:13 NASB)

> *That he would grant you, according to the riches of his glory, to be strengthened with might by his Spirit in the inner man; That Christ may dwell in your hearts by faith; that ye, being rooted and grounded in love…* (Eph 3:16-17)

> *If ye continue in the faith grounded and settled, and* be not moved away from the hope of the gospel, which ye have heard, and *which was preached to every creature which is under heaven; whereof I Paul am made a minister…* (Col 1:23)

> *And this word, Yet once more, signifieth the removing of those things that are shaken, as of things that are made, that those things which cannot be shaken may remain.* (Heb 12:27)
>
> *Whom resist stedfast in the faith, knowing that the same afflictions are accomplished in your brethren that are in the world.* (1 Pet 5:9)
>
> *Which hope we have as an anchor of the soul, both sure and stedfast, and which entereth into that within the veil...* (Heb 6:19)

No born-again person is a hostage to his experiences, memories, personality, or anything else that might engender soulishness. This does not mean Christians are to be emotionless; the Spirit provides the spiritual man with love, joy, empathy for others, and many other good and godly reactions and attitudes. But "freak-outs," "meltdowns," "venting," and other carnal displays are not of the Spirit of God but of the flesh. Jesus Christ set an example of displaying and utilizing the grace of God for Christians today; when his soul was troubled, He went away alone to communicate to the Father. Christians have the mind of Christ and by faith are to be as sound-minded, fearless, and unclouded as He. The spiritual Christian's mind has been well-described as being "unruffled" when he is operating by the power of the Spirit. Especially in contrast to the unattractive drama that characterizes the lives of so many, a stable mind and life is extraordinary!

Liberty

Now the Lord is that Spirit: and where the Spirit of the Lord is, there is liberty. (2 Cor 3:17)

The extraordinary life provided to the Christian includes liberty. The Law of Moses literally directed the steps of the Jewish people. Every part of life was ordered by its rules, from what they ate, to what they wore. The Christian, in contrast, is not bound in that way; he is free to make choices and has God's indwelling presence to give him wisdom. By using wisdom and the power of salvation, the spiritual man is able to live free from the commands of law without behaving lawlessly. He can do God's will without taking improper advantage of the fact that his sins have been paid in full. Handling one's liberty in a responsible way is an important part of spiritual maturity. The spiritual man can live free from the condemnation of the law, the dominion of sin, Satanic deception, and worldly enticements. He is also free to enjoy his life and make choices!

One man esteemeth one day above another: another esteemeth every day alike. *Let every man be fully persuaded in his own mind.* (Ro 14:5)

Let no man therefore judge you in meat, or in drink, or in respect of an holyday, or of the new moon, or of the sabbath days: Which are a shadow of things to come; but the body is of Christ. (Col 2:16-17)

Charge them that are rich in this world, that they be not highminded, nor trust in uncertain riches, but in the living God, who giveth us richly all things to enjoy… (1 Tim 6:17)

The Problem of Excluding Liberty

Not every Christian teacher emphasizes the blessing of liberty in Christ. In some cases this is due to a belief that liberty is an encouragement to sin. But liberty in Christ is not lawlessness, and it is certainly not for the purpose of indulging oneself. Liberty is primarily the freedom *not* to sin, but instead to do God's will, a choice that the unsaved do not have (Ro 6:20). This fact alone is extraordinary! Christian liberty is not licentiousness, a free-for-all, nor an opportunity to return to the bondage from which one was delivered. Liberty also includes making choices, freed from the strict limitations of the law. Liberty, however, has limits of its own; but how does a Christian know what he is free to do?

Firstly, one's liberty is to be considered within the parameters of the revealed will of God. A scripture that declares God's will on a particular matter indicates to the believer that failing to do it or doing the opposite does not fall within the bounds of liberty. An example of this is fornication; there is no case when sexual behavior outside of biblical marriage is approved by God. Secondly, the Christian must ask himself, can I do this as to the Lord? Liberty must be considered in light of one's own motives; only from a pure, God-honoring motive can a Christian legitimately exercise liberty. If something cannot be done as if it is being done for the Lord himself, it is not liberty. One cannot be a thief for the Lord, for example.

Because Christian liberty never leads to sin, a Christian must also evaluate whether a choice is likely to tempt him. If he falls into sin he is carnal, living like a natural man who can do nothing to please God; therefore, things which tempt him to sin are not part of liberty. The believer who uses liberty as an excuse to make choices which enslave him is deceived and carnal. Other considerations in regard to liberty include whether or not a particular choice is a good thing that edifies, whether it aids in maturity, and whether it might harm one's testimony or stumble a weaker believer (Ro 14:1-23, 1 Cor 8:8-13).

> *All things are lawful unto me, but all things are not expedient: all things are lawful for me, but I will not be brought under the power of any…all things are lawful for me, but all things edify not.* (1 Cor 6:12, 10:23b)

> *Stand fast therefore in the liberty wherewith Christ hath made us free, and be not entangled again with the yoke of bondage. … For, brethren, ye have been called unto liberty; only* use *not liberty for an occasion to the flesh, but by love serve one another.* (Gal 5:1, 13)

> *As free, and not using* your *liberty for a cloke of maliciousness, but as the servants of God.* (1 Pet 2:16)

Another reason that liberty is sometimes not emphasized is due to a low view of scripture, specifically regarding the Bible's claim to be sufficient for all things. What might be taught instead is to "seek" God's will for making choices. The danger in excluding the wise use of liberty as an option for making choices is that if something is not expressly addressed in scripture, where else can a Christian turn when attempting to make decisions? Perhaps there is someone who has faced a similar choice and can give advice, but there are many choices that cannot be directed by another person. A dilemma is created for the earnest Christian who wishes to do

God's will but finds no *directly* applicable scripture (i.e. "Should I move to Omaha?"). By excluding the freedom to simply make an informed choice, Christians might turn to seeking signs or feelings, which ushers them into the world of mysticism and soulishness. The Bible does not teach Christians to seek God's will, but to *do* God's will. The biblical record does not depict members of the early church wringing their hands and wondering what to do. Those who wished to obey God did what they knew they were to do, and apart from that they enjoyed freedom. The freedom to make choices does not reduce God's position or power in any way. He allows man to make choices within the limited scope of his small life; doing so does not impact God's plans for mankind or history. In the authors' opinion, what diminishes God is the belief that making a considered choice to move to Omaha somehow makes Him less powerful.

Having the liberty to choose does not, need not, and should not exclude God. James 1:5, for example, instructs the spiritual man to ask for wisdom. A believer might ask God to reveal a problem with a potential choice. Doing so does not guarantee a clear "answer" or a "peaceful feeling," but the earnest Christian can expect God to answer any prayer that is motivated by a desire to live in accordance with His will. There is a difference between asking God for help and assuming that an opportunity has been orchestrated by God. The former is godly dependence; the latter is akin to reading tea leaves. The spiritual man exercises maturity, wisdom, and common sense as he makes decisions, without making assumptions (Ja 4:15).

God is intimately involved in the lives of His children, but He does expect them to live as mature ones and not as trepidatious toddlers who must be directed every moment. He has provided a large book of instruction, unlimited access to wisdom, and the mind of Christ. He also provided the body of Christ, the members of which hold a wealth of biblical knowledge and life experience. The issue regarding liberty is that a Christian must not let his fear of making choices draw him into dangerous and immature practices which are absolutely not part of Christian living. Feelings can change on a whim, and signs can be counterfeited; an open door holds no guarantee that it is safe to walk through. Only God's word is completely trustworthy; furthermore, by its own testimony it is sufficient. Therefore, Christians are to be spiritual, ask for wisdom, search the scriptures for applicable principles or warnings, and then confidently make a choice. No feelings or signs are required. The scriptures do not promise that every choice will be right and every outcome will be wonderful. This is the nature of a mature relationship; sometimes choices are learning opportunities that enable one to make better decisions next time. Living with the consequences of choices, trusting God's word, and resting in contentment with whatever results is truly an extraordinary way to live.

Wisdom

If any of you lack wisdom, let him ask of God, that giveth to all men *liberally, and upbraideth not; and it shall be given him.* (Ja 1:5)

Access to the wisdom of God is another extraordinary aspect of the Christian life. God's wisdom is His truth applied. The better one knows God's word, the more ably one can live in accordance with His will. The Holy Spirit will illuminate a saint to apply known truths to his life. Even if an issue is not directly addressed in scripture, its general principles enable Christians to operate by faith and please God in everything they do.

Unlike prayers of intercession and supplication which might or might not be granted, requests for wisdom are always answered, "Yes!" All Christians can boldly ask for wisdom because God provides as much and as often as requested; He wants His wisdom to be utilized, for when it is, He is glorified.

That the God of our Lord Jesus Christ, the Father of glory, may give unto you the spirit of wisdom and revelation in the knowledge of him: The eyes of your understanding being enlightened; that ye may know what is the hope of his calling, and what the riches of the glory of his inheritance in the saints... (Eph 1:17-18)

For this cause we also, since the day we heard it, do not cease to pray for you, and to desire that ye might be filled with the knowledge of his will in all wisdom and spiritual understanding... (Col 1:9)

Let the word of Christ dwell in you richly in all wisdom... (Col 3:16a)

Walk in wisdom toward them that are without, redeeming the time. (Col 4:5)

But the wisdom that is from above is first pure, then peaceable, gentle, and *easy to be intreated, full of mercy and good fruits, without partiality, and without hypocrisy.* (Ja 3:17)

Proving

And be not conformed to this world: but be ye transformed by the renewing of your mind, that ye may prove what is that good, and acceptable, and perfect, will of God. (Ro 12:2)

The spiritual man is able to live in a way that is wise, stable, and free. The extraordinary God of the Bible even encourages His children to prove that this is so. He offers assurance that what He says is true, that He will do as He says, and that His program works perfectly for good. Proving the truth of God's word is not arrived at by tempting God and putting oneself into a bad situation in order to be rescued. It is accomplished when a Christian knows the truth, uses it, and finds that God's word proves itself: it really does work! The spiritual man proves God's word true as he receives answers to prayer, is content regardless of circumstances, tolerates suffering with astonishing patience, witnesses boldly, and trusts God in everything, looking with eagerness to the Savior's blessed appearing. When God's grace program is used, it is proven true to the believer himself and to all who witness his extraordinary life!

Proving what is acceptable unto the Lord. (Eph 5:10)

Prove all things; hold fast that which is good. (1 Thes 5:21)

But watch thou in all things, endure afflictions, do the work of an evangelist, make full proof of thy ministry. (2 Tim 4:5)

Notwithstanding the Lord stood with me, and strengthened me; that by me the preaching might be fully known (proven)... (Tim 4:17a, literal word added)

> *For the ministry of this service is not only fully supplying the needs of the saints, but is also overflowing through many thanksgivings to God. Because of the proof given by this ministry, they will glorify God for your obedience to your confession of the gospel of Christ and for the liberality of your contribution to them and to all...* (2 Cor 9:12-13 NASB)

A Few Other Examples

Even in the ordinary operations of life, Christians are to be extraordinary. For example, people need money to survive, and trusting one's income, savings and ability to earn is a natural mindset. A Christian, however, is not to think like a natural man. Because money is in many ways the equivalent of survival, desiring money can replace faith in God's provision. The oft repeated "money is the root of all evil" is actually more properly stated as "the love of money is a root for all sorts of evils." Conniving about ways to get money, stealing, other sorts of dishonest gain, selfishness, and a miserly lack of generosity are all examples of how the faithful fall into error.

> *But those who want to get rich fall into temptation and a snare and many foolish and harmful desires which plunge men into ruin and destruction. For the love of money is a root of all sorts of evil, and some by longing for it have wandered away from the faith and pierced themselves with many griefs.* (1 Tim 6:9-10 NASB)

> *Charge them that are rich in this world, that they be not highminded, nor trust in uncertain riches, but in the living God...* (1 Tim 6:17a)

Every man according as he purposeth in his heart, so let him give; *not grudgingly, or of necessity: for God loveth a cheerful giver.* (2 Cor 9:7)

Paul wrote that a Christian could give away every dime, but without love, it is nothing (1 Cor 13:3). This is because a Christian is to do all things as a spiritual man, and love is the principle product of spirituality. A grudging giver is giving carnally; his gift earns no reward and does not please God. A spiritual man who gives cheerfully has purposed in his own heart to advance God's will, and this glorifies God. God knows that people need to earn a living, save, and spend; within the bounds of liberty Christians can improve their financial situation and enjoy its fruits. They are simply warned not to covet money, feel superior for having it, or trust in it rather than trusting in God, who can give and take as He sees fit.

The same principle is true for other practical matters: Christians must know what the scripture teaches, and recognize that there is latitude. For example, the warning against yoking with an unbeliever in marriage allows Christians to marry for love, common interests, and shared goals, but it is foolish to even date a non-Christian. Once married, God wills that Christians remain married, trusting His sufficiency to cope with its ups and downs. When considering career options, selecting one that can be realistically had, can support a family, and that matches one's interests and skills is the wise way to go. Christians are free to move, but be sure there is a good church there. And if those who are closest express concerns about any choice, listen to them and take their concerns seriously. God is very practical and is not a micro-manager. It takes time and study to learn to use the mind of Christ and walk as a spiritual man. When it is appropriated, the results are extraordinary!

CHAPTER 8

GOD WILLS THAT CHRISTIANS HAVE EXTRAORDINARY RELATIONSHIPS

If we love one another, God abides in us, and his love is perfected in us. (1 Jhn 4:12b NASB)

Christians are the children of God through their second birth, a spiritual birth which imparts spiritual life. Being born again is accompanied by a "change in location" known as spiritual baptism: in the mind of God the believer is transferred from being "in Adam," the head of the human family, and placed "in Christ" as a member of His body, the church. The body of Christ is not a building, an activity, or an organization, but consists of the saints themselves. These two transactions—regeneration and spiritual baptism—create two new relationships: personal communion with God, and partnership among church members to achieve His aims.

Loving and Helping Believers

> *We are bound to thank God always for you, brethren, as it is meet, because that your faith groweth exceedingly, and the charity of every one of you all toward each other aboundeth…* (2 Thess 1:3)

Similar to the way that one loves and provides for one's biological family, the members of the spiritual family of God are to love and care for one another in practical ways. A necessity for believers of centuries past, this role of the church is greatly diminished in this age of plenty. In a conversation that the authors had with a professing Christian about this role, she said that it had never occurred to her to help other Christians, but instead assumed that "God would help them." That begs the question: "How does God help?" He did not need to create the church. Christians can worship, pray, study the Bible, and evangelize by themselves. But God does not instruct His children to live independently; He created a new and unique spiritual entity for two primary purposes: for the mutual benefit of its members, and for their service to one another to exemplify His love.

> *...but speaking the truth in love, we are to grow up in all* aspects *into Him who is the head,* even *Christ, from whom the whole body, being fitted and held together by what every joint supplies, according to the proper working of each individual part, causes the growth of the body for the building up of itself in love.* (Eph 4:15-16 NASB)

The spiritual and physical well-being of other Christians is to be a top priority of the church; each member is to be concerned with the betterment of the others. A properly functioning church body is an enemy to the operation of Satan and his world system, and, therefore, its members need one another for support, encouragement, friendship, instruction, correction, and for physical needs as well. Occupational ministers are to be well-provided for and the membership is to put one another above those outside the body. A local church which operates as a loving, helpful, trustworthy, and communicative family is better able to contend with worldly cares and troubles so that the work of evangelism is not hindered. When the church does not care for itself, its impact on the world is diminished.

> *And God is able to make all grace abound to you, so that always having all sufficiency in everything, you may have an abundance for every good deed; as it is written, "He scattered abroad, he gave to the poor, his righteousness endures forever." Now He who supplies seed to the sower and bread for food will supply and multiply your seed for sowing and increase the harvest of your righteousness; you will be enriched in everything for all liberality, which through us is producing thanksgiving to God. For the ministry of this service is not only **fully supplying the needs of the saints**, but is also overflowing through many thanksgivings to God.* (2 Cor 9:8-12 NASB)

> *For if the Gentiles have been made partakers of their spiritual things, their duty is also to minister unto them in carnal things* (earthly needs). (Ro 15:27b, clarification added)

> *The one who is taught the word is to share all good things with the one who teaches him.* (Gal 6:6 NASB)

> *Let the elders that rule well be counted worthy of double honour, especially they who labour in the word and doctrine.* (1 Tim 5:17)

Christians are to "do good unto all," but this is general decency and assistance in accordance with *God's* goals, not the "social gospel," a philosophy founded in a non-literal interpretation of scripture.

A local church can become quite unbalanced, providing little in terms of spiritual food, friendship, encouragement and physical aid to its members while emptying themselves for the sake of indifferent or even hostile unbelievers. If the world heard and saw the body of Christ teaching, serving, and truly loving one another as the early church did, it would have a very different opinion of "going to church" than it has today (Acts 5:13).

> *Distributing to the necessity of **saints**; given to hospitality.* (Ro 12:13)

> *And let us not be weary in well doing: for in due season we shall reap, if we faint not. As we have therefore opportunity, let us do good unto all* men, ***especially** unto them who are of the household of faith.* (Gal 6:9-10)

> *Praying us with much intreaty that we would receive the gift, and* take upon us *the fellowship of the ministering **to the saints**.* (2 Cor 8:4)

> *For God* is *not unrighteous to forget your work and labour of love, which ye have shewed toward his name, in that ye have ministered to the **saints**, and do minister.* (Heb 6:10)

> *Use hospitality **one to another** without grudging. As every man hath received the gift, even so minister the same **one to another**, as good stewards of the manifold grace of God.* (1 Pet 4:9-10)

Chapter 8: God Wills that Christians have Extraordinary Relationships

Hereby perceive we the love of God, *because he laid down his life for us: and we ought to lay down* our *lives for **the brethren**. But whoso hath this world's good, and seeth his brother have need, and shutteth up his bowels* of compassion *from him, how dwelleth the love of God in him?* (1 Jhn 3:16-17)

The term "brethren" means other Christians, referring to the fact that all believers are part of the family of God. So also, the phrase "one another" is a reference to those to whom the letters were written: the Christians. In Ephesians 4:16, Paul compared the body of Christ to a human body; all the members work together to provide for the operation of the other parts. He and the other writers of the epistles describe the many ways in which the members of the church are to be of benefit to one another, including love, aid, forgiveness, prayer, and unity. God wills that His children love one another and behave accordingly.

That their hearts might be comforted, being knit together in love, and unto all riches of the full assurance of understanding, to the acknowledgement of the mystery of God, and of the Father, and of Christ… (Col 2:2)

That they do good, that they be rich in good works, ready to distribute, willing to communicate (freely give as part of fellowship)… (1 Tim 6:18, clarification added)

Not forsaking the assembling of ourselves together, as the manner of some is; but exhorting one another: *and so much the more, as ye see the day approaching.* (Heb 10:25)

> *Beloved, let us love one another: for love is of God; and every one that loveth is born of God, and knoweth God. ... Beloved, if God so loved us, we ought also to love one another.* (1 Jhn 4:7, 11)
>
> *And now I beseech thee, lady, not as though I wrote a new commandment unto thee, but that which we had from the beginning, that we love one another.* (2 Jhn 1:5)
>
> *I will therefore that men pray every where, lifting up holy hands, without wrath and doubting* (disputing). (1 Tim 2:8, clarification added. To lift up hands in wrath is to lift them to fight. Christians are to lift their hands for holy purposes by using them to do what is right.)
>
> *And be ye kind one to another, tenderhearted, forgiving one another, even as God for Christ's sake hath forgiven you.* (Eph 4:32)
>
> *That there should be no schism in the body; but that the members should have the same care one for another.* (1 Cor 12:25)

All Christians are ministers, and primarily to one another in a visible outworking of the special love relationship among the members of God's family. This love bond among the saints is unique to the church. Through spirituality, God enables His children to sacrificially love one another, help one another, and to operate as one body in agreement and unity of purpose. The love and care that they provide one another is to be a display of the extraordinary nature of the love of God.

> *There is neither Jew nor Greek, there is neither bond nor free, there is neither male nor female: for ye are all one in Christ Jesus.* (Gal 3:28)
>
> *So we, being many, are one body in Christ, and every one members one of another.* (Ro 12:5)

God Wills That Christians Have a Sacrificial Attitude Toward Others

> *Let no one seek his own good, but that of his neighbor.* (1 Cor 10:24 NASB)

In direct contrast with the world's urging to put oneself first, the Bible teaches Christians to entrust themselves to God and endeavor to put first the well-being of others. Through the power of grace, Christians are to cast aside selfishness, over-concern for self-preservation, and the desire for preeminence. They are instead to live sacrificially for the sake of the salvation of others and the health of the church. God can be trusted; the child of God need not fear that he will lose or lack anything he needs by obeying his good and loving Father.

> *Let nothing be done through strife or vainglory; but in lowliness of mind let each esteem other better than themselves. Look not every man on his own things, but every man also on the things of others.* (Phil 2:3-4)
>
> *Be kindly affectioned one to another with brotherly love; in honour preferring one another…* (Ro 12:10)

> *We then that are strong ought to bear the infirmities of the weak, and not to please ourselves. Let every one of us please his neighbour for his good to edification.*
> (Ro 15:1-2)

Sacrifice is not foolish or extreme when viewed in light of what God has done out of love for mankind. God never asks His children to do anything to their detriment. Everything He wills is for good because He is always and only good. Everything that anyone has is something that was given or enabled by God; He has every right to expect that these gifts be used for His work and glory.

> *What? Know ye not that your body is the temple of the Holy Ghost which is in you, which ye have of God, and ye are not your own? For ye are bought with a price: therefore glorify God in your body, and in your spirit, which are God's.*
> (1 Cor 6:19-20)

> *Forasmuch as ye know that ye were not redeemed with corruptible things, as silver and gold, from your vain conversation received by tradition from your fathers; But with the precious blood of Christ, as of a lamb without blemish and without spot...* (1 Pet 1:18-19)

Living for the Lord and His priorities is necessary for both the proper functioning of the church and for its ministry to the world. The church includes people from every walk of life, different cultures, ideas, ways, means, and all manner of variations. Such a diverse group cannot cooperate nor be effective without the willingness to sacrifice in order to accomplish the work. Specific examples mentioned in scripture include sacrificing one's liberty for the sake of young or weak believers in order to avoid stumbling them. Younger Christians must respect and submit to the wisdom of elder Christians, sometimes sacrificing what they might prefer to do.

> *But take heed lest by any means this liberty of yours become a stumblingblock to them that are weak. … But when ye sin so against the brethren, and wound their weak conscience, ye sin against Christ.* (1 Cor 8:9, 12)

> *Let us not therefore judge one another any more: but judge this rather, that no man put a stumblingblock or an occasion to fall in* his *brother's way.* (Ro 14:13)

> *Likewise, ye younger, submit yourselves unto the elder. Yea, all* of you *be subject one to another, and be clothed with humility: for God resisteth the proud, and giveth grace to the humble.* (1 Pet 5:5)

> *…submitting yourselves one to another in the fear of God.* (Eph 5:21)

If a Christian believes that he is giving up something better in this world in order to obey God, then perhaps he does not understand God nor His purposes in grace. God's program has an eternal purpose and has no "down-side" other than some temporary trials meant for good. A sacrificial mindset is part of the divine viewpoint, and among its many benefits is the opportunity for extraordinary relationships.

Every Christian Is Called to Minister

God is faithful, by whom ye were called unto the fellowship of his Son Jesus Christ our Lord. (1 Cor 1:9)

Christian fellowship amounts to partnership; all Christians are called to participate in the ministry of reconciling to God those who are lost (2 Cor 5:18-19). The body of Christ is characterized as a body because its members are to operate in harmony and for mutual benefit, like the hand scratching an itch on the face and the eyes looking ahead for the stepping of the feet.

For we are labourers together with God... (1 Cor 3:9a)

Who also hath made us able ministers of the new testament... (2 Cor 3:6a)

Now then we are ambassadors for Christ... (2 Cor 5:20a)

But in all things approving ourselves as the ministers of God, in much patience, in afflictions, in necessities, in distresses... (2 Cor 6:4)

There is one body, and one Spirit, even as ye are called in one hope of your calling... (Eph 4:4)

Only let your conversation be as it becometh the gospel of Christ: that whether I come and see you, or else be absent, I may hear of your affairs, that ye stand fast in one spirit, with one mind striving together for the faith of the gospel... (Phil 1:27)

> *Wherefore the rather, brethren, give diligence to make your calling and election sure: for if ye do these things, ye shall never fall...* (2 Pet 1:10)

> *That which we have seen and heard declare we unto you, that ye also may have fellowship with us: and truly our fellowship* is *with the Father, and with his Son Jesus Christ.* (1 Jhn 1:3)

> *We therefore ought to receive such, that we might be fellowhelpers to the truth.* (3 Jhn 1:8)

Every Christian is called to minister to the needs of the body of Christ and to share the Gospel with the world. This partnership is another aspect of the extraordinary relationship that Christians have with God and one another.

Christians Can Agree

> *I am no longer in the world; and* yet *they themselves are in the world, and I come to You. Holy Father, keep them in Your name, the name which You have given Me, that they may be one even as We* are. ... *that they may all be one; even as You, Father,* are *in Me and I in You, that they also may be in Us, so that the world may believe that You sent Me. The glory which You have given Me I have given to them, that they may be one, just as We are one...* (Jhn 17:11, 21-22 NASB)

Agreement seems to have become scarce in many parts of life. When it is found, it might seem extraordinary, but it is to be ordinary within the church. Christ prayed that those who believed Him would be one, operating in unity and agreement. Was His prayer answered? Yes, it was. All those who are born from above already have spiritual unity, having been spiritually (not water) baptized (placed by the Holy Spirit) into Christ; through the implementation of grace doctrine, that spiritual unity is activated for practical use (Ro 6:3-13). Unity is vital to the effective operation of the church. There is no fellowship without agreement, no love in indifference, and no advancement of God's will amid division and strife.

Can two walk together, except they be agreed? (Amos 3:3)

The members of the church are called to be likeminded, and they can be when they are spiritual.

Be *of the same mind one toward another...* (Ro 12:16a)

Now the God of patience and consolation grant you to be likeminded one toward another according to Christ Jesus... (Ro 15:5)

Now I beseech you, brethren, by the name of our Lord Jesus Christ, that ye all speak the same thing, and that *there be no divisions among you; but* that *ye be perfectly joined together in the same mind and in the same judgment.* (1 Cor 1:10)

If there be *therefore any consolation in Christ, if any comfort of love, if any fellowship of the Spirit, if any bowels and mercies, Fulfil ye my joy, that ye be likeminded, having the same love,* being *of one accord, of one mind* (soul)... (Phil 2:1-2, literal word added. Note: "bowels" to the Hebrews was like "heart" to us, meaning affection and tenderness)

The result of being of "one mind," is spiritual fruitfulness, which produces other things such as courtesy, kind consideration, and cooperation. The practical unity that results from operating as spiritual men facilitates the work of the ministry for all members of the local church.

> *Finally, brethren, farewell. Be perfect, be of good comfort, be of one mind, live in peace; and the God of love and peace shall be with you.* (2 Cor 13:11)

> *Endeavouring to keep the unity of the Spirit in the bond of peace.* (Eph 4:3)

> *And to esteem them very highly in love for their work's sake.* And *be at peace among yourselves.* (1 Thes 5:13)

> *Finally,* be ye *all of one mind, having compassion one of another, love as brethren,* be *pitiful* (tender-hearted), be *courteous…* (1 Pet 3:8, synonym added)

Peace among believers and unity in the truth is for the cause of effectively spreading the salvation message as well as for mutual aid and comfort. God wills that Christians live out in practice the unity that He has already provided through Holy Spirit baptism into the body of Christ. When doctrinal disagreement affects unity, each must be willing to graciously correct and to be open to correction. There should be no greater desire in the heart of a Christian than to understand God's word rightly, as its truth and power is the wellspring for everything else in life. Those who want to know and understand it need only ask for illumination; that request will be answered affirmatively. God will even provide the desire to know His word (Phil 2:13)! Without teachable saints, God's will for the church is thwarted. Paul wrote that an unteachable mindset amounts to opposing oneself; the carnal man who refuses to acknowledge the truth makes himself the loser by becoming a vessel of dishonor.

> *Nevertheless the foundation of God standeth sure, having this seal, The Lord knoweth them that are his. And, Let every one that nameth the name of Christ depart from iniquity. But in a great house there are not only vessels of gold and of silver, but also of wood and of earth; and some to honour, and some to dishonour. If a man therefore purge himself from these, he shall be a vessel unto honour, sanctified, and meet for the master's use,* and *prepared unto every good work. Flee also youthful lusts: but follow righteousness, faith, charity, peace, with them that call on the Lord out of a pure heart. But foolish and unlearned questions avoid, knowing that they do gender strifes. And the servant of the Lord must not strive; but be gentle unto all* men, *apt to teach, patient, In meekness instructing those that oppose themselves; if God peradventure will give them repentance to the acknowledging of the truth;* (2 Tim 2:19-25)

The fact that millions of people of different ages, cultures, and times in history can all understand and believe the same thing, and work for the same purpose is truly extraordinary.

The Truth About Forgiveness

> *Forbearing one another, and forgiving one another, if any man have a quarrel against any: even as Christ forgave you, so also* do *ye.* (Col 3:13)

Chapter 8: God Wills that Christians have Extraordinary Relationships

All Christians sin. All Christians have been forgiven and on that basis are to forgive one another. Love and unity cannot exist without forgiveness among church members, both in humbly asking for it and in graciously giving it. The fact that some Christians refuse to forgive after a disagreement, wrongdoing, or an experience of hurt feelings is the most tragic of ironies. Unforgiveness is a scourge upon the church; it is a shame to the grudge-holder, a stumbling-block to others, and an outworking of faithlessness among those who themselves have been graciously forgiven. It is untrue to say, "I cannot forgive." God does not ask His children to do what they cannot. Forgiveness, however, might seem to be one of the most difficult aspects of the Christian life. Encountering the person to whom one owes forgiveness often triggers feelings which keep a Christian from believing that he is capable of forgiveness. No matter how one might try to justify unforgiveness, it is not an option for a Christian.

One of the difficulties regarding forgiveness might be that some Christians do not understand its exact nature. For example, some believe they cannot forgive because they cannot forget a wrong that was done to them. They do not realize that what they are called to do is not the same as what God does when He forgives. When God forgives, He sends sin away; He treats it as if it never happened (Heb 8:12, 10:17). Only He is capable of that and He does not ask human beings to do the same. Most people know from experience that intentionally "forgetting," as in the "forgive and forget" axiom, is nearly impossible. What Christians are asked to do instead is to use something that God has already provided.

The word translated forgiveness in regard to human beings is simply the word "grace." Grace is the empowering mechanism that enables God's will to be done. God has a gracious attitude toward sin: He forgives the sins of those who believe. Christians are to have His viewpoint and are, therefore, to be gracious when forgiveness is required. Living by the power of grace is to be the ordinary mode of operation anyway. When a Christian finds himself wronged, he is to operate the same way that he does in any case, extending undeserved favor and mercy. In short, one forgives by being spiritual and holy. Christian spirituality is the supernatural ability to emanate the character of God by faith in His promises, displaying the virtues of Jesus Christ. A person is unlikely to forget being wronged, but in refusing to set his mind upon it and instead direct faith toward the power of God, he can extend grace to others because God extended grace to him.

It is worth noting that forgiveness in the church is not that of Matthew 6:12, which is a conditional and legal requirement of the millennial kingdom; under kingdom law, one is forgiven *as* he forgives. In other words, he must forgive in order to be forgiven. Because of the work done on the cross by Jesus Christ, the Christian is already forgiven. He is, therefore, to extend grace to others whether or not they deserve it. In regard to the unsaved and/or unrepentant, there is no verse that excuses Christians from forgiveness. In other words, a Christian is not free to be ungracious because of the behavior of another. He does not minimize, excuse, accept, condone, approve of, or participate in the sin; neither does he allow himself to be misused or taken advantage of. He need not do anything at all for the carnal believer, but he is to maintain his Spirit-filled condition, being gracious rather than hostile, continuing to be available with the truth.

Chapter 8: God Wills that Christians have Extraordinary Relationships

> *Let all bitterness, and wrath, and anger, and clamour, and evil speaking, be put away from you, with all malice: And be ye kind one to another, tenderhearted, forgiving one another, even as God for Christ's sake hath forgiven you.* (Eph 4:31-32)

> *Bless them which persecute you: bless, and curse not. ... Recompense to no man evil for evil. Provide things honest in the sight of all men. If it be possible, as much as lieth in you, live peaceably with all men. Dearly beloved, avenge not yourselves, but* rather *give place unto wrath: for it is written, Vengeance* is *mine; I will repay, saith the Lord. Therefore if thine enemy hunger, feed him; if he thirst, give him drink: for in so doing thou shalt heap coals of fire on his head.* (Ro 12:14, 17-20)

In the case of an errant Christian, he is to be immediately returned to loving fellowship upon his repentance. Christian forgiveness is not simply mental assent, nor in word alone, but is a full restoration. For one to say that he forgives but in a practical way abandons his Christian brother has not fulfilled the call of grace. To fail in regard to this bedrock of Christianity is to make the goodness of Christ appear to be evil by allowing bitterness, hardness, or self-pity to replace grace. The church is to restore a repentant believer, and to do so with love.

> *Let not then your good be evil spoken of...* (Ro 14:16)

> *So that contrariwise ye* ought *rather to forgive* him, *and comfort* him, *lest perhaps such a one should be swallowed up with overmuch sorrow.* (2 Cor 2:7, referring to a Christian who was carnal but had since repented.)

> *Yet count* him *not as an enemy, but admonish* him *as a brother.* (2 Thes 3:15)

> *If thou count me therefore a partner, receive him as myself.* (Phm 1:17, referring to the believing slave who ran away.)

Restoring fellowship with a person after a falling-out might seem hopeless. Feelings change and memories remain. The Christian, however, is not to be ruled by his willful soul nor is he to dwell on the past. The emotions of the soul will align with God's viewpoint if the human spirit is renewed with truth. Unforgiveness cannot operate in communion with a God whose character is one of total forgiveness and love; the Christian harms and hardens himself by withdrawing or refusing to forgive. Each Christian must believe that he can do what God calls him to do, including forgive. To do so is another example of the extraordinary nature of Christian relationships when the saints operate according to God's will.

Debates and Fights Do Not Make Extraordinary Relationships

> *Even so the tongue is a little member, and boasteth great things. Behold, how great a matter a little fire kindleth! And the tongue is a fire, a world of iniquity: so is the tongue among our members, that it defileth the whole body, and setteth on fire the course of nature; and it is set on fire of hell. For every kind of beasts, and of birds, and of serpents, and of things in the sea, is tamed, and hath been tamed of mankind: But the tongue can no man tame; it is an unruly evil, full of deadly poison.* (Ja 3:5-8)

Chapter 8: God Wills that Christians have Extraordinary Relationships

James' letter to the churches contains strong warnings about the tongue. The tongue does more damage to relationships than perhaps anything else, and a debate can rapidly arouse a fit of bad temper and cause hard feelings. The good intentions with which one begins trying to convince another of the truth, or even of common sense, can easily escalate to utter exasperation and anger when there is disagreement. If someone is not open to truth, correction, or advice, trying to persuade him is not only a waste of time, but it can be potentially harmful, closing the door to future discussions. Protecting relationships with believers and unbelievers is more important than the immediate gratification of winning an argument; even a well-intentioned debater who desires that his opponent would be saved sometimes causes strife and ultimately accomplishes the opposite of what he intended. Debate is so problematic that it is listed among sins that most people would probably consider much more serious.

> *Being filled with all unrighteousness, fornication, wickedness, covetousness, maliciousness; full of envy, murder, debate, deceit, malignity; whisperers...* (Ro 1:29)

> *Receive one who is weak in the faith, but not to disputes over doubtful things.* (Ro 14:1 NKJV)

> *For I fear, lest, when I come, I shall not find you such as I would, and* that *I shall be found unto you such as ye would not: lest* there be *debates, envyings, wraths, strifes, backbitings, whisperings, swellings, tumults...* (2 Cor 12:20)

> *Let us walk honestly, as in the day; not in rioting and drunkenness, not in chambering and wantonness, not in strife and envying.* (Ro 13:13)
>
> *If any man teach otherwise, and consent not to wholesome words, even the words of our Lord Jesus Christ, and to the doctrine which is according to godliness; He is proud, knowing nothing, but doting about questions and strifes of words, whereof cometh envy, strife, railings, evil surmisings, Perverse disputings of men of corrupt minds, and destitute of the truth, supposing that gain is godliness: from such withdraw thyself.* (1 Tim 6:3-5)
>
> *Of these things put them in remembrance, charging them before the Lord that they strive not about words to no profit, but to the subverting of the hearers...* (2 Tim 2:14)
>
> *But avoid foolish questions, and genealogies, and contentions, and strivings about the law; for they are unprofitable and vain.* (Titus 3:9)

James describes the wise conduct which enables the spiritual man to testify and discuss while avoiding arguments, debates, and other disputes:

> *Wherefore, my beloved brethren, let every man be swift to hear, slow to speak, slow to wrath...* (Ja 1:19)

In order to do God's will, the spiritual man must maintain his fellowship with God by faith, thereby enabling him to produce the fruit of the Spirit. God's character emanates from the spiritual man; he exercises self-control and remains at peace. The supernatural ability to resist the temptation to argue or fight allows him to protect his relationships for future ministry opportunities. This is done out of love for others so that unbelievers may be saved and believers will not be stumbled. God provides extraordinary power which enables Christians to overcome their personalities, preferences, and tendencies in order to be Christlike in their relationships.

Let us therefore follow after the things which make for peace, and things wherewith one may edify another.
(Ro 14:19)

Humility and Submission to Authority

Submit yourselves to every ordinance of man for the Lord's sake: whether it be to the king, as supreme; Or unto governors, as unto them that are sent by him for the punishment of evildoers, and for the praise of them that do well.
(1 Pet 2:13-14)

Living in a free county and in a modern era facilitates high expectations in many areas of life. A typical Christian in America is likely to expect to eat every day, to sleep in a warm bed, to live according to his beliefs, and to a great degree to do as he likes. Human relationships are one part of life which often fail to meet expectations; they vary widely as to their quality and can be unpredictable. Marriages have their highs and lows; neighbors fall out of favor with one another over fences and yards, and friends come and go for many reasons. Nonetheless, Christian conduct is to be exemplary in all relationships, displaying Christlikeness regardless of the circumstances.

Dealing with those in authority can be among the most difficult of human interactions. Conflict with an authority is not simply personal but can affect one's career, one's finances, or even one's freedom. Those in authority and the rules they enforce are not always just, and yet the Bible calls Christians to submit to the powers of this world.

> *Let every soul be subject unto the higher powers. For there is no power but of God: the powers that be are ordained of God.* (Ro 13:1)

> *Put them in mind to be subject to principalities and powers, to obey magistrates, to be ready to every good work.* (Titus 3:1)

> Exhort *servants to be obedient unto their own masters,* and *to please* them *well in all* things; *not answering again...* (Titus 2:9)

> *Servants,* be *subject to* your *masters with all fear; not only to the good and gentle, but also to the froward* (obstinate). (1 Pet 2:18, synonym added)

In addition to governmental and occupational heirarchies, God has ordained authority in other relationships and parts of life, such as in marriage, in the church, and among age groups.

> *Wives, submit yourselves unto your own husbands, as unto the Lord.* (Eph 5:22, see also Col 3:18)

> *Let the woman learn in silence with all subjection. But I suffer not a woman to teach, nor to usurp authority over the man, but to be in silence.* (1 Tim 2:11-12)

Chapter 8: God Wills that Christians have Extraordinary Relationships

> *Likewise, ye younger, submit yourselves unto the elder. Yea, all of you be subject one to another, and be clothed with humility: for God resisteth the proud, and giveth grace to the humble.*
> (1 Pet 5:5, see also Eph 5:21)

Because the life of the Christian is to glorify God, it is worthwhile for a Christian to examine his attitude in regard to authority. Something as seemingly innocuous as breaking the speed limit is an act of rebellion against authority. A Christian might think that a rule or law is inconsequential, unfair, or foolish; this does not excuse him from obeying it. A minor violation might seem to be a small matter, but the greater issue is that of maturity. The maturity that develops from a spiritual response to authority will be of benefit in many other areas of life and set an example for other Christians. Humble submission is also part of the believer's identification with his Lord, who humbled Himself to the death of the cross.

> *And being found in fashion as a man, he humbled himself, and became obedient unto death, even the death of the cross.*
> (Phil 2:8)

No matter how circumstances might seem to justify independent action, there is never a valid reason to disobey God. His will is perfect and good, and those who allow themselves to be exercised by using grace teaching to develop humility and dependence upon God will experience His goodness more deeply and in more numerous ways. This is perhaps more recognizable in relationships than in any other area of life. One can be blessed with money, with opportunity, and with physical and mental gifts, but unrivaled is a blessed relationship. The Christian who is a blessing to those in authority over him are magnifying the name of Jesus Christ, giving credibility to their testimony, and bringing glory to God.

Other Scriptures on Social Interaction

The epistles describe the spiritual mindset and holy conduct of those who are indwelt by God. Readers are reminded that these teachings are not to be a stressful to-do list, but a standard against which the Christian can compare himself and readjust. For example, if a Christian recognizes in himself a desire to argue with his employer rather than to do as asked, he can renew his mind with a truth from scripture and immediately return to Spirit-filled operation, thinking and acting in accordance with God's will by God's power.

> *For it is God which worketh in you both to will and to do of his good pleasure.* (Phil 2:13)

In interpersonal relationships, Christians are to behave respectfully, with particular honor given to elder believers. Agedness in itself carries the wisdom of life experience.

> *Rebuke not an elder, but intreat* him *as a father; and the younger men as brethren; The elder women as mothers; the younger as sisters, with all purity. Honour widows that are widows indeed.* (1 Tim 5:1-3)

Christians are warned to be skeptical of accusations made against adult believers. If there are no other witnesses to an accusation, the information might be mere gossip or for the purpose of vengeance.

> *Against an elder receive not an accusation, but before two or three witnesses.* (1 Tim 5:19)

Christians are to resist partiality, which is the tendency to treat some believers better than others. It is the soul that has preferences. The human spirit, indwelt by God, recognizes value in each member of the body of Christ.

> *I charge thee before God, and the Lord Jesus Christ, and the elect angels, that thou observe these things without preferring one before another, doing nothing by partiality.* (1 Tim 5:21)

> *My brethren, do not hold the faith of our Lord Jesus Christ, the Lord of glory, with partiality.* (Ja 2:1 NKJV)

Christians are not to give their word or make a promise to another person unless they are certain they can and will keep it.

> *But above all, my brethren, do not swear, either by heaven or by earth or with any other oath; but* (unless) *your yes is to be yes, and your no, no, so that you may not fall under judgment.* (Ja 5:12 NASB, clarification added)

Disputes among Christians are to be resolved "in-house" whenever possible, so as not to shame the name of Christ. Paul insisted that it is better to be defrauded than to stain the reputation of the church. One person's public complaint defrauds other Christians by tarnishing their testimony through association. It helps to remember that earthly things are temporary, while those things which are done on Christ's behalf are eternal.

> *Dare any of you, having a matter against another, go to law before the unjust, and not before the saints? ... I speak to your shame. Is it so, that there is not a wise man among you? no, not one that shall be able to judge between his brethren? But brother goeth to law with brother, and that before the unbelievers. Now therefore there is utterly a fault among you, because ye go to law one with another. Why do ye not rather take wrong? why do ye not rather suffer yourselves to be defrauded? Nay, ye do wrong, and defraud, and that your brethren.* (1 Cor 6:1, 5-8)

The spiritual man believes that God will teach Him how to operate by faith and he studies God's word for that purpose. He compares his attitude and motive to the teachings of grace and adjusts himself accordingly. He looks to the promises of God with faith, and depends upon God to produce both the desire and ability to cooperate with Him. Such a man will be Christlike in his relationships and have priorities that put God's mission above personal gain or loss. He will treat others respectfully, submit to authority, forgive, love the brethren, work together without strife, and even sacrifice for them, because these are the natural results of spirituality. The Christian life is not a test as to whether or not the spiritual man can figure out God's will, nor a battle to dredge up enough personal willpower and "stick-to-itiveness" to follow through; it is a life of doing God's will as revealed in scripture, by the power of His grace, through simple faith in His promises. Extraordinary relationships will result.

> *He staggered not at the promise of God through unbelief; but was strong in faith, giving glory to God; And being fully persuaded that, **what he had promised,** he was able also to perform.* (Rom 4:20-21)

CHAPTER 9

SUFFERING AND GLORY

The elders which are among you I exhort, who am also an elder, and a witness of the sufferings of Christ, and also a partaker of the glory that shall be revealed... (1 Pet 5:1)

Suffering is a universal experience; it is the result of living in a fallen world cursed with sin. It is probably fair to say that most suffering is due to one's own sin and poor choices, and to the earthly conditions created by the sins of others. Christians suffer for other reasons also, and it might seem to be a contradiction that a loving Father in heaven allows it. Enduring suffering according to God's will is part of His greater plan to accomplish spiritual results within the believer, which ultimately brings Him glory.

> *Wherefore let them that suffer according to the will of God commit the keeping of their souls* to him *in well doing, as unto a faithful Creator.* (1 Pet 4:19)

Christians are appointed to suffering; it is part of a Christian's fellowship with his Lord. Christ suffered for the sins of the world, and the members of His body are equipped to bear it. Its purpose is for the spiritual man to be made "conformable unto his death," displaying Christ's virtues and character in times of hardship (Is 53:7, Luke 23:34).

> *For unto you it is **given** in the behalf of Christ, not only to believe on him, but also to suffer for his sake...*
> (Phil 1:29)

> *Yea doubtless, and I count all things but loss for the excellency of the knowledge of Christ Jesus my Lord... **That I may know him**, and the power of his resurrection, and the fellowship of his sufferings, being made conformable unto his death...*
> (Phil 3:8, 10)

> *That no man should be moved by these afflictions: for yourselves know that we are **appointed** thereunto.*
> (1 Thes 3:3)

> *Be not thou therefore ashamed of the testimony of our Lord, nor of me his prisoner: but be thou **partaker of the afflictions of the gospel** according to the power of God...*
> (2 Tim 1:8)

Chastening

One kind of suffering that a Christian might experience is chastening. Chastening is the divine response to a persistently unrepentant attitude toward sin. It might be due to intentional disobedience to the revealed will of God or unintentional disobedience due to intentional ignorance. Divine chastening is the spiritual equivalent of "child-training" by a parent, and its purpose is to turn the wayward saint from continuing in his ways. Chastisement is a necessity of God's justice; He did not save His children from condemnation with the world for the purpose of allowing them to practice ongoing sin without consequences.

Know ye not that ye are the temple of God, and that *the Spirit of God dwelleth in you? If any man defile the temple of God, him shall God destroy; for the temple of God is holy, which* temple *ye are.* (1 Cor 3:16-17)

But he that doeth wrong shall receive for the wrong which he hath done: and there is no respect of persons. (Col 3:25)

And ye have forgotten the exhortation which speaketh unto you as unto children, My son, despise not thou the chastening of the Lord, nor faint when thou art rebuked of him: For whom the Lord loveth he chasteneth, and scourgeth every son whom he receiveth. If ye endure chastening, God dealeth with you as with sons; for what son is he whom the father chasteneth not? But if ye be without chastisement, whereof all are partakers, then are ye bastards, and not sons. Furthermore we have had fathers of our flesh which corrected us, *and we gave* them *reverence: shall we not much rather be in subjection unto the Father of spirits, and live? For they verily for a few days chastened* us *after their own pleasure; but he for* our *profit, that* we *might be partakers of his holiness. Now no chastening for the present seemeth to be joyous, but grievous: nevertheless afterward it yieldeth the peaceable fruit of righteousness unto them which are exercised thereby.* (Heb 12:5-11)

For this cause many are *weak and sickly among you, and many sleep. For if we would judge ourselves, we should not be judged. But when we are judged, we are chastened of the Lord, that we should not be condemned with the world.* (1 Cor 11:30-32)

There is a progression in chastening which is meant to first slow the Christian's progress in his rebellion; if he persists, the consequences increase in severity. First is weakness, then sickness in order to deter further sin and bring about repentance. Early death can follow if the Christian does not cease from bringing shame to the name of Christ. Perhaps this is the source of the adage that "only the good die young," as chastening is for Christians only. Chastening can be avoided by self-judgment. The spiritual man who pauses throughout his day to "check-in with headquarters" can avoid sin by allowing the Holy Spirit to critique his thoughts and attitude. A few moments of quiet reflection on an applicable scripture can bring correction, ensuring that doubts, temptations, or desires do not lead to sin.

> *For the word of God is quick, and powerful, and sharper than any twoedged sword, piercing even to the dividing asunder of soul and spirit, and of the joints and marrow, and is a discerner of the thoughts and intents of the heart.* (Heb 4:12)

Persistently carnal Christians do not necessarily die prematurely; some are set aside because they are of no earthly use to the Lord. They are disqualified from Christian service and are instead allowed to live out the ultimate results of their choices.

> *But I discipline my body and bring it into subjection, lest, when I have preached to others, I myself should become disqualified.* (1 Cor 9:27 NKJV)

> *Examine yourselves* as to *whether you are* (operating) *in the faith. Test yourselves. Do you not know yourselves, that Jesus Christ is in you?—unless indeed you are disqualified.* (2 Cor 13:5 NKJV, clarification added)

> *They profess to know God, but in works they deny* Him, *being abominable, disobedient, and disqualified for every good work.* (Titus 1:16 NKJV; their works are burned: see Jhn 15:6, 1 Cor 3:15, Heb 6:8)

Not all carnality is visible, but the works of the flesh are manifest, meaning that one's sin is apparent (Gal 5:19). Fleshly manifestations can bring about discipline more swiftly than other sins due to their negative affect on one's testimony. It should not be assumed, however, that the illnesses or other physical ailments of a Christian are due to sin. A Christian can evaluate himself and know whether he is reaping the natural results of life such as aging, or of his own behavior such as poor diet and exercise habits, or whether he is being divinely chastened for sin.

Persecution

> *Yea, and all that will live godly in Christ Jesus shall suffer persecution.* (2 Tim 3:12)

Persecution for one's faith is the cause of some suffering. Suffering persecution for godly living is the one earthly, non-spiritual promise given to the church. The Christian who is living in a God-honoring manner, identifying closely with his Lord who was hated and rejected, will encounter similar attitudes and reactions in response to this manifestation of spirituality.

> *If the world hate you, ye know that it hated me before it hated you. If ye were of the world, the world would love his own: but because ye are not of the world, but I have chosen you out of the world, therefore the world hateth you. Remember the word that I said unto you, The servant is not greater than his lord. If they have persecuted me, they will also persecute you; if they have kept my saying, they will keep yours also. But all these things will they do unto you for my name's sake, because they know not him that sent me.* (Jhn 15:18-21)

> *I have given them thy word; and the world hath hated them, because they are not of the world, even as I am not of the world.* (Jhn 17:14)

> *For therefore we both labour and suffer reproach, because we trust in the living God, who is the Saviour of all men, specially of those that believe.* (1 Tim 4:10)

> *And they departed from the presence of the council, rejoicing that they were counted worthy to suffer shame for his name.* (Acts 5:41)

The experiences of suffering and joy are two things which are linked in the letters to the church. They might seem to be a strange pairing, but the joy which is produced by the indwelling Holy Spirit is not irrational gleefulness over something unpleasant; it is rather the calm joy of knowing that God is sufficient and faithful regardless of one's circumstances. The spiritual man experiences this comforting, calming joyfulness because he knows he has been counted worthy to attain further maturity in order to glorify God.

Great is my boldness of speech toward you, great is my glorying of you: I am filled with comfort, I am exceeding joyful in all our tribulation. (2 Cor 7:4)

Trials and Tribulations

For verily, when we were with you, we told you before that we should suffer tribulation; even as it came to pass, and ye know. (1 Thes 3:4)

Many of the trials of life are simply an unpleasant but rather ordinary part of earthly existence such as financial, family, or health problems. The experience of suffering in life's trials offers the spiritual man an opportunity to mature by enduring them in a God-honoring way. A tribulation is a particular type of trial that facilitates maturity because it cannot be escaped. The one suffering a tribulation can do nothing but wait for it to pass. For example, a person might have a financial trial that can be escaped or minimized with a bank loan or a gift from a family member. But if the problem is a serious injury, he can only wait for the healing process; there is nothing else to be done about it. The believer who goes through tribulation as a spiritual man, trusting God to sustain him, will develop patience and experience. God's faithfulness in comforting and strengthening the believer through the suffering creates the confident expectation that God is faithful in time of trouble. Because his hope in God is not confounded but rather proven true, his trust in and dependence upon God grows, and his heart is flooded with love for God:

> *By whom also we have access by faith into this grace wherein we stand, and rejoice in hope of the glory of God. And not only so, but we glory in tribulations also: knowing that tribulation worketh patience; And patience, experience; and experience, hope: And hope maketh not ashamed* (does not confound); *because the love of God is shed abroad in our hearts by the Holy Ghost which is given unto us.* (Ro 5:2-5, clarification added)
>
> *Rejoicing in hope; patient in tribulation; continuing instant in prayer...* (Ro 12:12)
>
> *These things I have spoken unto you, that in me ye might have peace. In the world ye shall have tribulation: but be of good cheer; I have overcome the world.* (Jhn 16:33)
>
> *And so, after he had patiently endured, he obtained the promise.* (Heb 6:15)

In times of future need, the confident expectation (hope) in God that resulted from the tribulation encourages the believer to approach Him boldly and receive well-timed help:

> *Let us therefore come boldly unto the throne of grace, that we may obtain mercy, and find grace to help in time of need.* (Heb 4:16)

In the naturally-occurring trials of life, such as loss due to death, God wills that His children should not sorrow as those who have no hope. God understands and comforts his children as they grieve, empowering them to endure. A Christian need not "fall apart" nor dwell endlessly upon the loss. Such self-focus does not glorify

God, give hope to others, nor help one's testimony. The spiritual man's expectation is that God will deal justly with the departed, comfort the grieving believers, and use the loss to bring eternity to mind in those who do not believe. This is how calm, confident joy comes from sorrow.

> *But I would not have you to be ignorant, brethren, concerning them which are asleep, that ye sorrow not, even as others which have no hope. For if we believe that Jesus died and rose again, even so them also which sleep in Jesus will God bring with him.* (1 Thes 4:13-14)

> *Take, my brethren, the prophets, who have spoken in the name of the Lord, for an example of suffering affliction, and of patience. Behold, we count them happy which endure. Ye have heard of the patience of Job, and have seen the end of the Lord; that the Lord is very pitiful* (full of pity for us; compassionate), *and of tender mercy.* (Ja 5:10-11, clarification added)

A Christian's response to trials, temptations, and suffering is part of what determines his reward. The difficult experiences in life and the thrill of being rewarded for enduring them in a way that pleases God causes the spiritual man to love the promise of Christ's return.

> *That the trial of your faith, being much more precious than of gold that perisheth, though it be tried with fire, might be found unto praise and honour and glory at the appearing of Jesus Christ...* (1 Pet 1:7)

> *We ought always to give thanks to God for you, brethren, as is only fitting, because your faith is greatly enlarged, and the love of each one of you toward one another grows ever greater; therefore, we ourselves speak proudly of you among the churches of God for your perseverance and faith in the midst of all your persecutions and afflictions which you endure. This is a plain indication of God's righteous judgment so that you will be considered worthy of the kingdom of God, for which indeed you are suffering.* (2 Thes 1:3-5 NASB)

> *He that hath an ear, let him hear what the Spirit saith unto the churches; To him that overcometh will I give to eat of the tree of life, which is in the midst of the paradise of God. ... Fear none of those things which thou shalt suffer: behold, the devil shall cast some of you into prison, that ye may be tried; and ye shall have tribulation ten days: be thou faithful unto death, and I will give thee a crown of life.* (Rev 2:7, 10)

> *Blessed is the man that endureth temptation: for when he is tried, he shall receive the crown of life, which the Lord hath promised to them that love him.* (Jas 1:12)

> *Henceforth there is laid up for me a crown of righteousness, which the Lord, the righteous judge, shall give me at that day: and not to me only, but unto all them also that love his appearing.* (2 Tim 4:8)

The letters to the church mention affliction, suffering, and trials quite often. Some trials are for the purpose of testing. These are to be precious to the spiritual man because they try his faith in order to purify it. For example, when one is reproached for his righteousness or wrongfully accused, and yet handles it graciously, he is displaying the grace that Jesus Christ displayed in his earthly ministry (Jn 1:14).

> *For this* is *thankworthy, if a man for conscience toward God endure grief, suffering wrongfully. For what glory* is it, *if, when ye be buffeted for your faults, ye shall take it patiently? but if, when ye do well, and suffer* for it, *ye take it patiently, this* is *acceptable with God. For even hereunto were ye called: because Christ also suffered for us, leaving us an example, that ye should follow his steps…* (1 Pet 2:19-21)

> *Beloved, think it not strange concerning the fiery trial which is to try you, as though some strange thing happened unto you: But rejoice, inasmuch as ye are partakers of Christ's sufferings; that, when his glory shall be revealed, ye may be glad also with exceeding joy. If ye be reproached for the name of Christ, happy* are ye; *for the spirit of glory and of God resteth upon you: on their part he is evil spoken of, but on your part he is glorified.* (1 Pet 4:12-14)

> *And he said unto me, My grace is sufficient for thee: for my strength is made perfect in weakness. Most gladly therefore will I rather glory in my infirmities, that the power of Christ may rest upon me. Therefore I take pleasure in infirmities, in reproaches, in necessities, in persecutions, in distresses for Christ's sake: for when I am weak, then am I strong.* (2 Cor 12:9-10)

Because He trusted God, Paul rejoiced in his suffering. He knew that everything that God allowed was for his good. He realized that those experiences drew him to more consistent fellowship with God and taught him to walk in dependence upon the power of God's grace. He valued that much more than the short-term benefit of escaping the unpleasant circumstances. The unusual reaction of spiritual Christians to suffering often provides another benefit: questions from observers which are an opportunity to explain one's hope (confident expectation) in Christ. Notice that the following passage does not say that one should try to act happy, or try to make oneself happy, or figure out some way to be happy in trials. The suffering believer *is* happy. He is suffering because he has been righteous, pleasing his Lord and bringing Him glory. He is happy because he is spiritual and is therefore able to view his situation from God's perspective. He remembers that the trial is temporary and that the return of the Lord is near. His spiritual condition and his identification with his savior are the reasons for his happiness, even as he is suffering.

> *But and if ye suffer for righteousness' sake, happy* are ye: *and be not afraid of their terror, neither be troubled; But sanctify the Lord God in your hearts: and* be *ready always to give an answer to every man that asketh you a reason of the hope that is in you with meekness and fear: Having a good conscience; that, whereas they speak evil of you, as of evildoers, they may be ashamed that falsely accuse your good conversation in Christ. For it is better, if the will of God be so, that ye suffer for well doing, than for evil doing.* (1 Pet 3:14-17; note: this passage does not teach Christians to wait to share the Gospel until someone asks.)

Abundant Comfort

In regard to the suffering of His people, God is good, loving, kind, and just. He does not allow His children to suffer without providing the means to cope. The call to fellowship includes the coordination of self-care; as a person would care for a family member or his own physical body, the saints are to provide practical help and emotional support as needed. Pastors and teachers play a vital role, educating the members about their many spiritual benefits and how to use them. The love expressed among the members of the body in trials, tribulation, and other types of suffering is another provision that God has made for His children; it is also a testimony to the world.

> *That is, that I may be comforted together with you by the mutual faith both of you and me.* (Ro 1:12)

> *Rejoice with them that do rejoice, and weep with them that weep.* (Ro 12:15)

> *But he that prophesieth* (proclaims what God has said) *speaketh unto men* to *edification, and exhortation, and comfort.* (1 Cor 14:3, clarification added)

> *That there should be no schism in the body; but* that *the members should have the same care one for another. And whether one member suffer, all the members suffer with it; or one member be honoured, all the members rejoice with it.* (1 Cor 12:25-26)

> *That their hearts might be comforted, being knit together in love...* (Col 2:2a)

> *Wherefore comfort one another with these words.* (1 Thes 4:18)
>
> *Wherefore comfort yourselves together, and edify one another, even as also ye do.* (1 Thes 5:11)

The church does not utilize the Law of Moses for daily operation; nonetheless, the Old Testament scriptures are important and useful for the church. Its historical accounts teach its readers about God's compassionate and trustworthy character. The narratives of God's dealings with the Jewish people and others show His great care, mercy, and longsuffering toward mankind. A Christian who knows the faithful character of his gracious God can face the trials of life with patience and confident assurance, treasuring the joyful expectation of a future with Him. The spiritual man knows that Jesus Christ—his God, creator, and friend—died to provide the hope of that glorious day.

> *For whatsoever things were written aforetime were written for our learning, that we through patience and comfort of the scriptures might have hope* (a confident expectation).
> (Ro 15:4, clarification added)

In addition to support from the body of Christ and the comfort of the Old Testament scriptures, God has provided supernatural spiritual comfort. He sent the Holy Spirit to aid the spiritual man in his sorrows. The Holy Spirit illuminates, teaches, and brings to remembrance those truths which are needed so that he can utilize the wisdom and spiritual bounty that God has provided. As he sets his mind on the truths of scripture, he is comforted. He can also go to God in prayer, pouring out his cares to the Lord who loves him.

> *And I will pray the Father, and he shall give you another Comforter, that he may abide with you for ever; ... I will not leave you comfortless: I will come to you. ... But the Comforter,* which is *the Holy Ghost, whom the Father will send in my name, he shall teach you all things, and bring all things to your remembrance, whatsoever I have said unto you.* (Jhn 14:16, 18, 26)

> *Casting all your care upon him; for he careth for you.* (1 Pet 5:7)

> *Then had the churches rest throughout all Judaea and Galilee and Samaria, and were edified; and walking in the fear of the Lord, and in the comfort of the Holy Ghost, were multiplied.* (Acts 9:31)

Since the fall in Eden's garden, humanity has suffered and struggled. God's curse upon the earth was just, and His gracious provision for deliverance from it is available to all, by faith. Those who believe the Gospel of Christ, 1 Corinthians 15:1-4, are God's children, and although He allows suffering for the purpose of maturity, He knows that "growing up" is difficult. His practical and supernatural comfort and encouragement, administered through His saints, His word, and the Holy Spirit Himself, works to stabilize the believer so that he is not swallowed up by the sorrows of this world.

> *So that contrariwise ye* ought *rather to forgive* him, and comfort him, *lest perhaps such a one should be swallowed up with overmuch sorrow.* (2 Cor 2:7)

> *Blessed be the God and Father of our Lord Jesus Christ, the Father of mercies and God of all comfort, who comforts us in all our affliction so that we will be able to comfort those who are in any affliction with the comfort with which we ourselves are comforted by God. For just as the sufferings of Christ are ours in abundance, so also our comfort is abundant through Christ. But if we are afflicted, it is for your comfort and salvation; or if we are comforted, it is for your comfort, which is effective in the patient enduring of the same sufferings which we also suffer; and our hope for you is firmly grounded, knowing that as you are sharers of our sufferings, so also you are sharers of our comfort.* (2 Cor 1:3-7 NASB)

God's comfort enables the spiritual man to maintain a proper perspective when suffering, reminding him of life's purpose, its brevity, and the glorious deliverance that is to come.

> *And if children, then heirs; heirs of God, and joint-heirs with Christ; if so be that we suffer with* him, *that we may be also glorified together. For I reckon that the sufferings of this present time are not worthy to be compared with the glory which shall be revealed in us.* (Ro 8:17-18)

> *For our light affliction, which is but for a moment, worketh for us a far more exceeding and eternal weight of glory…* (2 Cor 4:17)

> We are *troubled on every side, yet not distressed;* we are *perplexed, but not in despair; Persecuted, but not forsaken; cast down, but not destroyed; Always bearing about in the body the dying of the Lord Jesus, that the life also of Jesus might be made manifest in our body.* (2 Cor 4:8-10)

> *But in all* things *approving ourselves as the ministers of God, in much patience, in afflictions, in necessities, in distresses, In stripes, in imprisonments, in tumults, in labours, in watchings, in fastings; ... As sorrowful, yet alway rejoicing; as poor, yet making many rich; as having nothing, and* yet *possessing all things.* (2 Cor 6:4-5, 10)

Glorifying God: The Other Side of Suffering

> *Yet if* any man suffer *as a Christian, let him not be ashamed; but let him glorify God on this behalf.* (1 Pet 4:16)

The purpose of the Christian life is to bring glory to God, and there is perhaps no greater opportunity to show forth the beautiful virtues of Jesus Christ than when one is suffering. The Christian who bears up under suffering and handles it graciously without bitterness, grumbling, blame, and other works of the flesh, is displaying the power of the grace of God which indwells him. Paul described this spiritual objective in 2 Cor 4:10: "...that the life of Jesus might be made manifest in our body." Emanating God's character is always the result of spirituality, and suffering in particular can display the vast difference between the spiritual man who has access to hope and peace, and the natural man who might feel nothing other than anger, fear, or grief. A godly response to suffering of any kind comes not from will-power but from faith. The believer looks to the promises of God in grace and asks himself, for example, "Do I believe that God will produce these responses in me? Can I really experience peace, contentment, and the calm joy of completely trusting Him even when I am suffering? Do I believe God even when circumstances are bad? Is my desire to glorify God regardless of my situation?" A brief self-evaluation can return the hurting Christian to the power of God's spiritual deliverance from the feelings of desperation, exasperation, hopelessness, or defeat which often accompany trials. The natural man has no reason to glorify God in suffering. The spiritual man has endless reasons to glorify God regardless of his circumstances.

> *That ye may with one mind* and *one mouth glorify God, even the Father of our Lord Jesus Christ.* (Ro 15:6)
>
> *That, according as it is written, He that glorieth, let him glory in the Lord.* (1 Cor 1:31)
>
> *Whether therefore ye eat, or drink, or whatsoever ye do, do all to the glory of God.* (1 Cor 10:31)
>
> *That we should be to the praise of his glory, who first trusted in Christ.* (Eph 1:12)
>
> *Unto him* be *glory in the church by Christ Jesus throughout all ages, world without end. Amen.* (Eph 3:21)
>
> *When he shall come to be glorified in his saints, and to be admired in all them that believe (because our testimony among you was believed) in that day. Wherefore also we pray always for you, that our God would count you worthy of this calling, and fulfil all the good pleasure of his goodness, and the work of faith with power:* **That the name of our Lord Jesus Christ may be glorified in you***, and ye in him, according to the grace of our God and the Lord Jesus Christ.* (2 Thes 1:10-12)

> *Whereunto he called you by our gospel, to the obtaining of the glory of our Lord Jesus Christ.* (2 Thes 2:14)

> *Now unto the King eternal, immortal, invisible, the only wise God,* be *honour and glory for ever and ever. Amen.* (1 Tim 1:17)

> *Having your conversation honest among the Gentiles: that, whereas they speak against you as evildoers, they may by your good works, which they shall behold, glorify God in the day of visitation.* (1 Pet 2:12)

> *Now unto him that is able to keep you from falling, and to present* you *faultless before the presence of his glory with exceeding joy, To the only wise God our Saviour,* be *glory and majesty, dominion and power, both now and ever. Amen.* (Jude 1:24-25)

Suffering is not something Christians desire; it might even seem to be a worthless experience. To cope with suffering, the spiritual man reminds himself that one of God's primary objectives is to do a work within him. Suffering trains him to look away from his circumstances and instead believe in the sufficiency of the grace-through-faith system. The Christian who turns to his Lord for shelter in life's storms will grow in faith, develop wisdom to help others, and lean on the Lord in other circumstances as well. He will also be a godly example to others as he allows the power of God's grace to bring him through it with quiet dignity and self-control. The members of the body of Christ are being prepared to rule and reign with Him. If suffering is what is needed to drive the believer to the scriptures and prayer, God allows it. The Christian who cooperates with God through the trials of life brings Him glory. Amen.

CHAPTER 10

GOD WILLS THAT CHRISTIANS' LIVES BE PROFITABLE, NOW AND IN THE FUTURE

> *That ye may be blameless and harmless, the sons of God, without rebuke, in the midst of a crooked and perverse nation, among whom ye shine as lights in the world; Holding forth the word of life; that I may rejoice in the day of Christ, that I have not run in vain, neither laboured in vain.* (Phil 2:15-16)

Every born-again believer is counted righteous from the moment of regeneration. When he places his faith for salvation in the Gospel of Christ, 1 Corinthians 15:1-4, the righteousness of Christ is imputed to him; this means that in the mind of God, it is counted as his. As the Christian learns God's word and aligns his viewpoint, attitude, and motives with God's, his spiritual condition enables him to act rightly. His life and relationships reflect God's grace and purpose as he works in fellowship with the body of Christ, brings the Gospel to the lost, and generally does good rather than evil. All that he does, whether ministry-related or not, is done with consideration to his spiritual condition. The spiritual man knows that works performed by the power of the flesh are not profitable and will burn when tested (1 Cor 3:11-15, Heb 6:7-8).

The Fruits of Righteousness

> *And God is able to make all grace abound toward you; that ye, always having all sufficiency in all things, may abound to every good work...* (2 Cor 9:8)

God wills that His children do good, and many verses encourage "good works." Doing good works by faith can be difficult to understand. Many Christians, the authors included, initially tend to believe that faith is something needed only for those things which are unknown, difficult, or seemingly impossible. It is vital for Christians to learn that grace-through-faith is to be the manner of daily operation. Only the spiritual man is able to act in accordance with the righteousness that he already possesses and produce good works. For example, a Christian might find his workday to be hectic. He wants to go home and just relax, but he knows his family will need things from him. He takes a moment to evaluate his inner man and recognizes that he is irritated and exhausted. He remembers that God promises to strengthen him, to provide peace, and to enable a quiet (serene, tranquil, unruffled) spirit. He asks himself if he believes these promises of scripture. He acknowledges that they are true, and God immediately produces these within him. Grace empowers him to deal patiently and efficiently with things at home, leaving him some time to relax as well. His service to his family is counted as a good work by God because it resulted from faith.

> *Now he that ministereth seed to the sower both minister bread for your food, and multiply your seed sown, and increase the fruits of your righteousness...* (2 Cor 9:10)

Being filled with the fruits of righteousness, which are by Jesus Christ, unto the glory and praise of God. (Phil 1:11)

But ye, brethren, be not weary in well doing. (2 Thes 3:13)

But What Am I Supposed to Do?

Some good works are as humble as chores around the house and some are as risky as witnessing to a co-worker; what matters in the grace-through-faith system is not the magnitude of the task but the spiritual condition in which it is produced. It is God's work in the spiritual man which makes his works righteous and consequently of a quality that glorifies Him. It is vastly more important that a Christian learns to live by faith as a spiritual man than that he keeps busy doing what he believes to be good works. He who tries to perform by the power of his flesh will at least become weary, and having left the enabling power of the Spirit, he could find himself in a condition worse than weariness.

In addition to the ordinary tasks of daily life, all Christians are to share the Gospel message, be of help to the body of Christ, communicate to God, study and teach His word, and live a holy, God-honoring life. Beyond these necessities for spirituality and for the operation of the church, a Christian has much liberty. He has choices about what to do with his life and how he will serve as a minister of Christ. He should exercise wisdom as to what to do and take into consideration things such as practicality, financial means, situation in life, individual talents and abilities, preferences, and the needs of others within one's sphere of influence. For example, he might recognize that witnessing to foreign people who reside in the United States can be much more easily accomplished than traveling to a foreign country to witness, and he is free to do either.

Training one's own children in the truth from an early age can potentially bear more fruit than almost anything else one can do. And few people can say they have no neighbor, friend, or family member who could benefit from their spiritual understanding and willingness to serve. God will make good use of those who are willing to cooperate with Him and carry out His grace program as revealed in scripture.

> *For we are his workmanship, created in Christ Jesus unto good works, which God hath before ordained that we should walk in them.* (Eph 2:10)

> *In like manner also, that women adorn themselves in modest apparel, with shamefacedness and sobriety; not with broided hair, or gold, or pearls, or costly array; But (which becometh women professing godliness) with good works.* (1 Tim 2:9-10)

> *That they do good, that they be rich in good works, ready to distribute, willing to communicate* (freely give as part of fellowship)... (1 Tim 6:18)

> *All scripture is given by inspiration of God, and is profitable for doctrine, for reproof, for correction, for instruction in righteousness: That the man of God may be perfect, throughly furnished unto all good works.* (2 Tim 3:16-17)

> *Who gave himself for us, that he might redeem us from all iniquity, and purify unto himself a peculiar people, zealous of good works.* (Titus 2:14)

> *Put them in mind to be subject to principalities and powers, to obey magistrates, to be ready to every good work…*
> (Titus 3:1)

> *This is a faithful saying, and these things I will that thou affirm constantly, that they which have believed in God might be careful to maintain good works. These things are good and profitable unto men. … And let ours also learn to maintain good works for necessary uses, that they be not unfruitful.*
> (Titus 3:8, 14)

> *And let us consider one another to provoke unto love and to good works…* (Heb 10:24)

> *Make you perfect in every good work to do his will, working in you that which is wellpleasing in his sight, through Jesus Christ; to whom be glory for ever and ever. Amen.* (Heb 13:21)

Christians do not need to invent good works and projects to do. The spiritual man will recognize opportunities to do good in everyday life. The presence of a Christian should improve the tenor of a conversation, the productivity of a work place, and the joyfulness of a gathering, and nobody should wonder why. Christians are not to do good works to make others wonder why they did them. It should be obvious and clear by his verbal testimony and matching behavior that a Christian does good rather than make mischief because he is a witness on behalf of the good God of the Bible. The spiritual man is a profitable employee, spouse, neighbor, and friend, bringing benefit to those in his life. Every word and work of a spiritual man is a display of the love and goodness of Jesus

Christ Himself, and is for the purpose of blessing the brethren and sharing the good news of Christ's death, burial, and resurrection for sin with the lost.

Now our Lord Jesus Christ himself, and God, even our Father, which hath loved us, and hath given us everlasting consolation and good hope through grace, Comfort your hearts, and stablish you in every good word and work. (2 Thes 2:16-17)

*For God so loved the world, that he gave his only begotten Son, that whosoever believeth in him should not perish, but have everlasting life. For God sent not his Son into the world to condemn the world; but that the world through him might be saved. He that believeth on him is not condemned: but he that believeth not is condemned already, because he hath not believed in the name of the only begotten Son of God. And this is the condemnation, that light is come into the world, and men loved darkness rather than light, because their deeds were evil. For every one that doeth evil hateth the light, neither cometh to the light, lest his deeds should be reproved. But he that **doeth truth** cometh to the light, that his deeds may be made manifest, **that they are wrought in God**.* (Jhn 3:16-21)

God Wills Abundant Spiritual Life for His Spiritual People, the Church

The good and wonderful God of the Bible is in no way miserly; everything the believer has in Christ has been provided abundantly with nothing lacking. It is according to God's will that His children are fully equipped to do all that He asks, and that they are heaped to overflowing with His love, grace, mercy, and forgiveness. Through familiarity with God's written word and faith in His illuminating and enabling power, the spiritual man can learn and apply what he has in Christ and enjoy the abundance that was provided through Jesus' sacrifice on the cross. The fact that this life includes suffering does not contradict God's promise of a spiritually abundant life. It is in knowing and appropriating by faith one's spiritual blessings that one is able to bear up under suffering. God has already given the saints all that His grace provides:

> *Blessed* be *the God and Father of our Lord Jesus Christ, who hath blessed us with all spiritual blessings in heavenly* places *in Christ…* (Eph 1:3)

> *I am come that they might have life, and that they might have it more abundantly.* (Jhn 10:10b)

> *For if by one man's offence death reigned by one; much more they which receive abundance of grace and of the gift of righteousness shall reign in life by one, Jesus Christ.* (Ro 5:17)

> *For all things* are *for your sakes, that the abundant grace might through the thanksgiving of many redound to the glory of God.* (2 Cor 4:15)

> *Now unto him that is able to do exceeding abundantly above all that we ask or think, according to the power that worketh in us…* (Eph 3:20)

> *Not by works of righteousness which we have done, but according to his mercy he saved us, by the washing of regeneration, and renewing of the Holy Ghost; Which he shed on us abundantly through Jesus Christ our Saviour...* (Titus 3:5-6)

> *Blessed be the God and Father of our Lord Jesus Christ, which according to his abundant mercy hath begotten us again unto a lively hope by the resurrection of Jesus Christ from the dead...* (1 Pet 1:3)

> *For so an entrance shall be ministered unto you abundantly into the everlasting kingdom of our Lord and Saviour Jesus Christ.* (2 Pet 1:11)

The world, the flesh, and the devil are all trying to thwart the Christian's profitability to God. God wills that His children walk in freedom from these enemies, and He has enabled them to do so. The Christian life is sometimes characterized as a race, and the carnal Christian who does not use the provision of grace, but rather succumbs to his enemies, might be disqualified from this race. His life choices and lack of growth make him unusable for the work for which his savior purchased him. His salvation is intact, but his rewards are lost and his life brings no glory to the Lord that bought him.

> *But none of these things move me, neither count I my life dear unto myself, so that I might finish my course with joy, and the ministry, which I have received of the Lord Jesus, to testify the gospel of the grace of God.* (Acts 20:24)

> *Do you not know that those who run in a race all run, but only one receives the prize? Run in such a way that you may win. Everyone who competes in the games exercises self-control in all things. They then do it to receive a perishable wreath, but we an imperishable. Therefore I run in such a way, as not without aim; I box in such a way, as not beating the air; but I discipline my body and make it my slave, so that, after I have preached to others, I myself will not be disqualified* (useless for service)*.* (1 Cor 9:24-27 NASB)

> *Wherefore seeing we also are compassed about with so great a cloud of witnesses, let us lay aside every weight, and the sin which doth so easily beset* us, *and let us run with patience the race that is set before us, Looking unto Jesus the author and finisher of* our *faith; who for the joy that was set before him endured the cross, despising the shame, and is set down at the right hand of the throne of God.* (Heb 12:1-2)

> *If a man therefore purge himself from these, he shall be a vessel unto honour, sanctified, and meet for the master's use,* and *prepared unto every good work.* (2 Tim 2:21)

> *For ye are bought with a price: therefore glorify God in your body, and in your spirit, which are God's.* (1 Cor 6:20)

The Christian's reward is not the impoverished things of this world which moth and rust destroy (Mt 6:19-20); they are things which have everlasting consequences. There is a reason that there will be tears in heaven when those who shunned God's offer of reward finally see what could have been accomplished for God's glory if only the meager and temporary things of this world had been cast aside.

> *While we look not at the things which are seen, but at the things which are not seen: for the things which are seen* are *temporal; but the things which are not seen* are *eternal.* (2 Cor 4:18)

> *Brethren, I count not myself to have apprehended: but* this *one thing* I *do, forgetting those things which are behind, and reaching forth unto those things which are before, I press toward the mark for the prize of the high calling of God in Christ Jesus.* (Phil 3:13-14)

Or Despisest Thou the Riches of His Goodness…? (Ro 2:4a)

The Bible teaches that what Christians have in Christ are true riches. In order to bring glory to God by accessing the full benefit of salvation, the spiritual man must view his salvation and all that accompanies it as precious riches. He treats it accordingly and works it out generously, even to his own detriment for the sake of the Gospel.

> *In whom we have redemption through his blood, the forgiveness of sins, according to the riches of his grace; … The eyes of your understanding being enlightened; that ye may know what is the hope of his calling, and what the riches of the glory of his inheritance in the saints…* (Eph 1:7, 18)

> *Unto me, who am less than the least of all saints, is this grace given, that I should preach among the Gentiles the unsearchable riches of Christ; … That he would grant you, according to the riches of his glory, to be strengthened with might by his Spirit in the inner man…* (Eph 3:8, 16)

> *But my God shall supply all your need according to his riches in glory by Christ Jesus.* (Phil 4:19)
>
> *To whom God would make known what is the riches of the glory of this mystery among the Gentiles; which is Christ in you, the hope of glory...* (Col 1:27)
>
> *That in every thing ye are enriched by him, in all utterance, and in all knowledge...* (1 Cor 1:5)
>
> *As sorrowful, yet alway rejoicing; as poor, yet making many rich; as having nothing, and yet possessing all things.* (2 Cor 6:10)
>
> *Being enriched in every thing to all bountifulness, which causeth through us thanksgiving to God.* (2 Cor 9:11)
>
> *For ye know the grace of our Lord Jesus Christ, that, though he was rich, yet for your sakes he became poor, that ye through his poverty might be rich.* (2 Cor 8:9)
>
> *I counsel thee to buy of me gold tried in the fire, that thou mayest be rich; and white raiment, that thou mayest be clothed, and that the shame of thy nakedness do not appear; and anoint thine eyes with eyesalve, that thou mayest see.* (Rev 3:18)

There is even more to good works than the blessing it brings to others and the glory it brings to God. God wants eternal profit to be another result of salvation! What He offers should never be diminished or treated with disdain. The reward of the inheritance in the next life is something every Christian is to strive for and count as precious, as it is another blessing that Jesus died to provide.

> *Hearken, my beloved brethren, Hath not God chosen the poor of this world rich in faith, and heirs of the kingdom which he hath promised to them that love him?* (Ja 2:5)

> *That in the ages to come he might shew the exceeding riches of his grace in his kindness toward us through Christ Jesus.* (Eph 2:7)

Profit Motive

Profit and reward are mentioned often in the epistles. The most valuable benefit of one's salvation is the privilege of sharing the good news with others.

> *Even as I please all men in all things, not seeking mine own profit, but the profit of many, that they may be saved.* (1 Cor 10:33)

Good works are only profitable to the doer if they are the product of spirituality, the primary characteristic of which is love:

> *And though I bestow all my goods to feed the poor, and though I give my body to be burned, and have not charity* (love), *it profiteth me nothing.* (1 Cor 13:3, synonym added)

There is literally no profit, meaning no reward, for a good work done by a Christian who does not know how to operate as a spiritual man. It is not uncommon for a person to put enormous effort into his family, career, lifestyle, amusements, and his own body. Paul compares such things with the profitability of a God-honoring life, putting them into perspective by offering God's viewpoint:

> *For bodily exercise profiteth little: but godliness is profitable unto all things, having promise of the life that now is, and of that which is to come.* (1 Tim 4:8)

The author of Hebrews expects the Christian to put significant effort into his spiritual life:

> *That ye be not slothful, but followers of them who through faith and patience inherit the promises.* (Heb 6:12)

> *For consider him that endured such contradiction of sinners against himself, lest ye be wearied and faint in your minds. Ye have not yet resisted unto blood, striving against sin.* (Heb 12:3-4)

The grace-through-faith system empowers the spiritual man to do God's will. The only alternative is to operate in the flesh, energized by the principle (law) of sin; doing so brings no reward and the result is counted by God as sin, even if the world considers it to be a good deed.

> *Because the carnal mind* is *enmity against God: for it is not subject to the law of God, neither indeed can be. So then they that are in the flesh cannot please God.* (Ro 8:7-8)

> *…for whatsoever* is *not of faith is sin.* (Ro 14:23b)

> *But without faith* it is *impossible to please* him*: for he that cometh to God must believe that he is, and* that *he is a rewarder of them that diligently seek him.* (Heb 11:6)

Don't Fall

> *Behold, I Paul say unto you, that if ye be circumcised, Christ shall profit you nothing. ... Christ is become of no effect unto you, whosoever of you are justified by the law; ye are fallen from grace.* (Gal 5:2, 4)

To fall from grace means to fail to use the grace-through-faith system. Because he is operating apart from grace, the carnal Christian's salvation is presently of no effect; he is operating as if he is a natural (unsaved) man. He might not be doing exactly the same things as he did before he was saved, but he is functioning independently of God rather than by faith; consequently, he is not able to please God. His spiritual birth (regeneration) cannot be reversed, but its benefits are being wasted.

The church to whom James wrote suffered from many interpersonal problems, including the rich members mistreating and refusing to help those who were poor. Because of their spiritual immaturity, their faith was not profitable in daily living; it did not produce anything of value. In the context of being saved from the temptation to sin, James explains that the daily walk of faith cannot help anyone if it is "dead," meaning separated from its purpose. Like a dead body separated from its spirit, faith that produces nothing is equally useless. Without faith in the promises of God, a Christian cannot live free from the dominion of sin nor fulfill God's will. When faith is used as intended, it is "made perfect," a reference to Christian maturity.

> *What* doth it ***profit***, *my brethren, though a man say he hath faith, and have not works? can faith save him* (from temptation and sin described in James 1)? *If a brother or sister be naked, and destitute of daily food, And one of you say unto them, Depart in peace, be* ye *warmed and filled; notwithstanding ye give them not those things which are needful to the body; what* doth it ***profit***? *Even so faith, if it hath not works, is dead, being alone* (separated from its purpose). *Yea, a man may say, Thou hast faith, and I have works: shew me thy faith without thy works, and I will shew thee my faith by my works. … But wilt thou know, O vain man, that faith without works is dead* (useless, unprofitable)? *… Seest thou how faith wrought with his works, and by works was faith made perfect? … For as the body without the spirit is dead, so faith without works* (the expected outworking of faith) *is dead also.* (Ja 2:14-18, 20, 22, 26, clarification added)

The ordinary activities and interactions of life can lead the spiritual man into carnality if he is not diligent to evaluate his spiritual condition as he goes about his day. Even small things can be stumbling blocks if a Christian is not alert. Consider the fact that the members of the church in James' epistle were fighting about where to sit (Ja 2:3)! The things that one gets drawn into can waste time, damage one's testimony, negatively impact others, and most importantly, rob God of the glory that He deserves. They are unprofitable.

> *But avoid foolish questions, and genealogies, and contentions, and strivings about the law; for they are unprofitable and vain.* (Titus 3:9)

The Christian who determines to do God's will and utilizes His spiritual provision is richly rewarded! He blesses those to whom he ministers, enjoys the supernatural peace and joy of spirituality, and glorifies God on judgment day! His greatest reward will be the opportunity to use the spiritual understanding that he gained in his earthly life to ably rule and reign with Jesus Christ in His kingdom.

> *If any man's work abide which he hath built thereupon, he shall receive a reward.* (1 Cor 3:14)

> *And when the chief Shepherd shall appear, ye shall receive a crown of glory that fadeth not away.* (1 Pet 5:4)

> *For if I do this thing willingly, I have a reward...* (1 Cor 9:17a)

> *For we must all appear before the judgment seat of Christ; that every one may receive the things done in his body, according to that he hath done, whether it be good or bad.* (2 Cor 5:10)

> *Knowing that of the Lord ye shall receive the reward of the inheritance: for ye serve the Lord Christ.* (Col 3:24)

> *Cast not away therefore your confidence, which hath great recompence of reward. For ye have need of patience, that, after ye have done the will of God, ye might receive the promise.* (Heb 10:35-36)

> *Look to yourselves, that we lose not those things which we have wrought, but that we receive a full reward.* (2 Jhn 1:8)

And from Jesus Christ, who is *the faithful witness,* and *the first begotten of the dead, and the prince of the kings of the earth. Unto him that loved us, and washed us from our sins in his own blood, And hath made us kings and priests unto God and his Father; to him* be *glory and dominion for ever and ever. Amen.* (Rev 1:5-6)

To him that overcometh will I grant to sit with me in my throne, even as I also overcame, and am set down with my Father in his throne. (Rev 3:21)

And hast made us unto our God kings and priests: and we shall reign on the earth. (Rev 5:10)

Blessed and holy is *he that hath part in the first resurrection: on such the second death hath no power, but they shall be priests of God and of Christ, and shall reign with him a thousand years.* (Rev 20:6)

How gracious is our God! How perfect is His will! How wonderful are His ways! May every believer read all about it and believe what is written so that he might be profitable to God, bringing Him glory and honor into the ages. Amen.

CONCLUSION

WHAT GOD'S WILL IS NOT

Wherefore be ye not unwise, but understanding what the will of the Lord is. (Eph 5:17)

When Christians consider God's will, it is likely to be part of a decision about things like marriage, a job, a house, or a move. Answers to these questions, however, are noticeably absent from scripture. God says His word is sufficient, and yet we know that it addresses general principles such as "marry a Christian," and not specific choices, such as "Don't marry Forest." The Christian spiritual life, while commonly thought of as a clean or moral lifestyle, is not essentially about making good earthly decisions; it is about doing everything by the power of the Holy Spirit. It is less about the particulars of earthly life, but rather about operating consistently as a spiritual man, looking in faith to the Lord for the right attitude, motive, and supernatural empowerment to live each day for the glory of God. The Christian who uses God's grace-through-faith operating system will make better choices than the one who does not.

God's will under grace allows for significant latitude and freedom; Christians are to use biblical understanding and spiritual wisdom to make decisions as mature sons. Without recognizing the nature of God's will, one is left with either law: "You can do this, but not that," or mysticism: "What do I think God is telling me?" Perhaps it is a misunderstanding of how blessings are imparted under grace that has led many Christians to anguished hand-wringing, fearful of making a choice contrary to God's will. Therefore, it is worth stating again: God has spoken. He revealed His will through the Apostles and New Testament prophets who recorded it for posterity, laying the foundation of the church which need not be laid again. By its own testimony, God's written word is sufficient for all things pertaining to life and godliness. Therefore, since it does not say, "Bill, buy a house," we can conclude that Bill is free, and that scripture is sufficient to enable Bill to make a wise choice.

Thinking about God's will in this way might be very new to some readers. It takes time to absorb spirituality after having spent one's Christian life trying to live by "do's and don'ts." In learning what something is, we, the authors, have always found it helpful to describe what it is not. In contrast to what scripture teaches about God's will, here are some things that God's will is not:

- Not an experience, although living in accordance with it produces experiences such as peacefulness, joyfulness, contentment, and thankfulness.
- Not a feeling or a "sense" of something.
- Not a whisper, or a message, or a voice, ideas which are taught nowhere in scripture, but sprang from a poor rendering of 1 Kings 19:12.
- Not necessarily an open door; Satan can open doors and so can personal determination.
- Not a predetermined plan for one's life.
- Not an assumption that whatever happens is "meant to be." Most things that happen in this world are contrary to God's will.

- Not a "give-to-get" system. We already have everything in grace.
- Not a bait-and-switch program as in the axiom "He closes a door and opens a window."
- Not necessarily a lesson. Although we can learn from operating according to God's will, the lessons we need are already in the Bible; God does not set us up to fail, for example, so that we can learn a lesson. Neither does the Bible teach that every experience is a lesson or that everything that happens in life has a particular meaning.

Furthermore, God's word does not promise "confirmation," of a choice made. Taking a feeling, experience, sign, or comment from someone else and arbitrarily assigning it the exalted status of being a confirmation from God is never even suggested to the church. The demonic spirit realm, however, will gleefully provide things to keep Christians away from the scripture and looking in all the wrong places.

> *But I fear, lest by any means, as the serpent beguiled Eve through his subtilty, so your minds should be corrupted from the simplicity that is in Christ.* (2 Cor 11:3)

The teaching that God sends private messages to Christians about whether to go left or right on the various roads in life has led to an epidemic of claims which amount to God contradicting His own word. If He is now revealing micro-directives to millions of individuals, it is a vast departure from the record of the scriptures which teach that He has already made known His will. He has called His revelation to man sufficient, preserving it in writing through the centuries and stating that nothing should ever be added. Has this "new way" of attempting to live the Christian life improved the church? In our opinion, it has not. The calling of God is sure because it is written. In order to mature in the faith and benefit from grace, each Christian must decide whether or not he believes the record of scripture, which includes its claim of sufficiency to the exclusion of all else. One cannot spiritually mature, fulfill God's will, and at the same time reject teachings from the Bible.

A belief in divine revelation through feelings, dreams, signs, or similar things might begin as passive watchfulness, but it can lead a Christian into the treacherous territory of seeking these things. Therefore, we include a warning: Seeking spiritual information, guidance or understanding beyond what God has provided is called "divination." It is an occult practice which is forbidden by scripture and is very dangerous (Deut 18:10-15, 2 Kings 17:17-18, 21:6). The lure of personalized information draws the heart of man *away* from God (Deut 13:1-5) and can result in unwanted and terrifying encounters with the spirit world (1 Sam 16:14). God considers any effort to gather information apart from His revelation to be rebellion (1 Sam 15:23). If a person believes he has received extra-biblical revelation, this should be a cause for concern. If he is not born-again, he does not have the protective seal of the Holy Spirit and can become possessed by the spirit who is communicating with him. Christians who become entangled in supernatural encounters cannot be possessed, but they can become deceived and be a source of deception to others. Christians are to cling to the safe harbor of the written word and believe God who declares that He provides His children with everything needed (2 Cor 9:8, Phil 4:19). If this seems not to be so, the solution is not to search outside the Bible but to do further research within it.

Testimonies of the miraculous can also lead Christians astray, causing doubt in regard to the sufficiency of God's word. A miracle is an event that defies natural law and is, therefore, of supernatural origin. God does indeed do miraculous things and actively intervenes in the lives of His children. However, people from all religions have had experiences that are supernatural or at least seem so. Non-Christians receive things they have prayed for and have doors of opportunity open for them. As shown in the Bible, some miracles and wonders come from God and some do not (Ex 7:11, 7:22, 8:7, Mt 7:22-23, Acts 16:16, Rev 13:13-14, 16:14). There are powers in the heavenlies that can make all kinds of things happen on earth, and the most deceptive things are those which appear to be good. The issue in regard to Christian living is this: one cannot know for certain the source of supernatural occurrences and it is not necessary to know. Trusting in anything apart from the written word of God is a potential doorway to deception. False religion and mysticism are like slot machines; they pay off just often enough to keep people playing.

> *For such are false apostles, deceitful workers, transforming themselves into the apostles of Christ. And no marvel; for Satan himself is transformed into an angel of light. Therefore it is no great thing if his ministers also be transformed as the ministers of righteousness; whose end shall be according to their works.* (2 Cor 11:13-15)

There are also practical reasons to heed the warning against extra-biblical revelation. Some who make claims about knowing God's will in regard to specific personal decisions must shamefacedly reveal later that they made the wrong choice. Whether due to a job they disliked, a fiancé who turned out to be a poor match, or an open door that subsequently hit them on the back, those who find themselves back-peddling after touting a claim about "God's will" find it a humiliating experience. The claimant soon realizes that his choice was an ordinary human mistake.

The consequences of making claims on behalf of God can be dire, and looking foolish is the least of these. One can damage one's testimony, appear to be a liar, stumble other believers, and cause others to doubt God. An idea that comes to mind might make you wonder if it came from God, but it is wiser to resist the temptation to assume or claim that it did. The spiritual man continually renews his mind with the truths of scripture so that he is not drawn off-course by random ideas. Furthermore, feelings are certainly not a reliable confirmation; they can change with the weather, a song on the radio, or a cup of coffee. The good news is that God does not have to use unreliable methods such as imperfect human reasoning, changing circumstances, and fickle feelings. His word, rightly divided, works every time.

Damaged faith is another common result of trusting signs, open doors, or personal thoughts and feelings to determine God's will. For example, a person who made an unfortunate job change might express anger toward God because, "He put me here." But did He? Who was it that applied, accepted the job, packed, and moved? What might one conclude about God after He supposedly revealed His "will" and then nothing worked out as expected? Is God fickle? Perhaps He is not all-knowing and He made an error? God did not make this person do what he did, and yet because he made the claim, God gets the blame. Will this person's faith in God remain the same after blaming Him for an unhappy outcome? It should be apparent that claims of perceived revelation from God can damage one's faith as well as God's name. Some reverse course after a mistaken decision, spending time and money undoing what they just did. Others feel obligated to stay the course. Injured pride, embarrassment, commitments made, financial consequences, and reputational harm are among the reasons that some remain stuck for years in a situation of their own making. The Christian must always do ordinary earthly homework and use his God-given intellect and spiritual wisdom to make decisions rather than depending upon a feeling, private thought, or some other so-called sign or "confirmation."

Satan is to blame for some cases of decisions gone wrong; after all, he is the god of this age. He can open and close doors and affect many events on this planet. In other cases, one's own desire is enough to get the ball rolling to bring something to pass and then personal determination and perseverance take it the rest of the way. There is nothing wrong with working toward a goal; the issue is not to claim to know that it is God's will apart from biblical revelation. We know that God intervenes in the affairs of this world, but many things in life are simply due to natural consequences; for example, a person has the needed skills, applies for a job, and gets hired. Any job can be done in accordance with God's will; no special dispensation is required to please Him. The spiritual man can glorify God with his integrity, work ethic, customer service, reliability, and many other Spirit-produced virtues, as well as with his efforts to share the Gospel of Christ. God is not more or less glorified by the earthly particulars but by the condition of the inward man. Whether he is making an ordinary daily decision or taking a seemingly miraculous opportunity, it is the Spirit-filled Christian who pleases God in all that he does.

Grace doctrine does not instruct us to find God's will, but to know and understand it. Because Christians are to do God's will, we know that His will is readily available. Because the revelation of God's will has been written down, it is much the same for us all. We, the authors, completely understand that it seems more special to believe that God is personally delivering a customized plan. But isn't liberty enough? Do we so under-appreciate the glorious liberty of the sons of God that there is no delight in having been given choices? Consider the tribes of Israel which suffered under the burden of 613 laws! The entirety of creation is longing to enjoy the liberty that the spiritual man already has. Walking free from sin and enjoying deliverance from superstition, fear, and the cares of this world by using the mind of Christ is a blessing beyond words. A Spirit-filled Christian can do nearly anything he wants with his life, all with God's blessing, because his inward condition will produce that which is pleasing to God. Having already been given all spiritual blessings in the heavenlies, a Christian is not going to get "more" because of moving to the "right" city or selecting the "right" house. There are certainly earthly blessings to be had by making wise choices. But there is not only one choice to be had. We can marry any available adult Christian of the opposite sex, work in an occupation that we enjoy, and move to an interesting city, assured that we are in the will of God because we are operating as spiritual men!

Each Christian has a personal and intimate relationship with God; that relationship is informed by the Bible and nothing else. It does

Conclusion: What God's Will is Not

not teach that there is only one decision which suits God and that we must hunt to discover it, as if it is a cosmic game of hide-and-seek. We can and certainly should pray for God to be involved in all our decisions. We can ask Him to provide opportunities and help, but that is not the same as claiming to know that He did. God is to be given the glory for everything good, and thanked even when things are not so good, but we, the authors, ask our readers to please refrain from presuming and claiming to know what God is or is not doing, apart from His written revelation.

Similarly, the exhausting and frustrating exercise of trying to discover "lessons" in life events amounts to a religious version of pin-the-tail-on-the-donkey. The Bible does not state that there is a lesson in every experience. It is God's will that we learn, but the lessons He wishes to teach us are written in the Bible. While our experiences can teach us much, God's word promises that all we need to know from Him has already been provided. He has not shorted anyone, nor has He created a system in which we must sin and fail in order to learn. Consistent spirituality facilitates maturity, enabling the spiritual man to grow in his understanding of how to apply grace doctrine. The Bible is perfect and complete by its own testimony. Each must decide if he believes it, but if a lesson is desired, here it is: in every situation Christians are to learn the same thing—to know God better and to trust Him more.

Dear Christian, rest easy when you have decisions to make. You have been placed in an exalted position in Christ, something that even the heroes of the faith did not enjoy (Heb 11:39-40). You are already special in all the universe, and you will always be in God's will if you are operating in accordance with that position by living as a spiritual man. When you are rightly adjusted to the Spirit of

God, you cannot be otherwise. God's word has stood the test of time; for twenty centuries it has been leading the saints in wisdom and righteousness. Cling to it and renew your mind with the truth; this will allow you to discern your motives and actions and make wise choices. Both in ordinary human life and in spiritual life, one cannot mature without the freedom to make choices. If your choice is not selfish, sinful, or foolish, you very likely have liberty to make that choice. God gave us limits within which to exercise our liberty. We have a very practical God, and a not-at-all mystical God. He wrote down all that we need for life and godliness, and gave us the mind of Christ to understand it, the intellectual sense for things not addressed, and each other—a wealth of wisdom among the members of the body of Christ. Believe it and enter into His rest. Amen.

Let us be glad and rejoice, and give honour to him...
(Rev 19:7a)

Notes

Notes

Notes

About the Authors

Preston Condra and his wife Kelly serve in independent, full-time Christian ministry. Preston graduated from Oklahoma Baptist University and Southwestern Baptist Theological Seminary. His lifelong service has included preaching across the country, teaching, lecturing, writing, and appearing on broadcasts. Kelly has been speaking and teaching throughout her career. The Condras share a passion for the Gospel of Christ, found in 1 Corinthians 15:1–4. Through their ministry, *Sufficient Word,* they teach, preach, and offer training in evangelism and discipleship. They have co-authored and published many books, producing practical materials to help Christians share their faith and grow in grace. Through *By the Book Design and Book Management,* a consulting service, they help authors to professionally publish their books: *www.bythebook.design.*

www.sufficientword.com

www.ingramcontent.com/pod-product-compliance
Lightning Source LLC
Chambersburg PA
CBHW050315120526
44592CB00014B/1920